THE MESSAGES WORKBOOK

Powerful Strategies for Effective Communication at Work & Home

Martha Davis, Ph.D. • Kim Paleg, Ph.D. • Patrick Fanning

New Harbinger Publications, Inc.

Publisher's Note

This publication is designed to provide accurate and authoritative information in regard to the subject matter covered. It is sold with the understanding that the publisher is not engaged in rendering psychological, financial, legal, or other professional services. If expert assistance or counseling is needed, the services of a competent professional should be sought.

Distributed in Canada by Raincoast Books

Copyright © 2004 by Martha Davis, Patrick Fanning, and Kim Paleg
New Harbinger Publications, Inc.
5674 Shattuck Avenue
Oakland, CA 94609
www.newharbinger.com

Cover images by Digital Vision/Getty Images

Cover design by Amy Shoup

Acquired by Catharine Sutker

Edited by Brady Kahn

Text design by Tracy Marie Carlson

ISBN 1-57224-349-X Paperback

19   18   17

15   14   13   12   11   10   9   8

Contents

Introduction   1

PART I
Laying the Groundwork for Effective Communication

CHAPTER 1
Listening: How to Really Hear What Others Have to Say   7

CHAPTER 2
Opening Up: When, What, and to Whom to Disclose about Yourself   25

CHAPTER 3
Expressing Yourself: Creating Clear and Effective Messages   35

PART 2
Handling Difficult Conversations and Situations

CHAPTER 4
Regulating Your Emotions: Managing Intense Anger   51

CHAPTER 5
Asserting Yourself: The Middle Way between Aggressive and Passive Styles   63

CHAPTER 6
Fighting Fair: How to Disagree with Intimates   77

CHAPTER 7
Negotiating Conflict: Winning without Intimidating or Caving In   89

CHAPTER 8
Holding Your Own: Coping with Differences in Power   103

CHAPTER 9
Dealing with Strong Emotions: Communicating with People in Pain   115

PART 3
Out in the World: Friends, Family, and Work

CHAPTER 10
Sensitizing Yourself to Gender: Understanding the Opposite Sex   129

CHAPTER 11
Making Contact: Meeting New People and Cultivating Friendships   145

CHAPTER 12
Discussing Sex: Getting Past Inhibitions and Communicating Your Needs   157

CHAPTER 13

Talking with Children: Understanding Kids and Making Sure They Understand You   169

CHAPTER 14

Talking with Teens: Bridging the Generation Gap   187

CHAPTER 15

Talking with Elders: Maintaining Contact with Aging Family Members   199

CHAPTER 16

Making a Difference: Communicating in Small Groups   209

CHAPTER 17

Overcoming Stage Fright: Speaking Effectively in Public   221

References   231

Introduction

You need adequate communication skills just to survive in life. The better your communication skills, the happier you will be. You'll make friends more easily. You'll find a life partner more easily. Good communication helps in raising kids, getting through school, finding work, making money, and participating in your community.

If you don't communicate well, you are always at a disadvantage. When you fail to express your ideas clearly and forcefully, other people's ideas prevail. When you can't express your feelings, your feelings get hurt. When you can't ask for what you want, you don't get it.

Most people learn their communication skills from their parents, with lessons coming later from friends and teachers. If your parents, teachers, and friends were poor role models, this book will fill some gaps in your communication skills.

WHY A WORKBOOK?

Unlike many self-help books that are *about* communication, this book *teaches* communication skills. Good communication is a skill, like dancing, riding a bike, or remembering the times tables. It improves with practice. By doing the exercises in this workbook, you learn by doing, which is the most effective way of acquiring a new skill or improving an existing skill.

When you read a chapter, it's okay to skim through and see what it's all about. But to really learn the skills in a chapter, you have to go back and do the exercises. Only by completing the checklists, coming up with the answers, filling in your own personal information, and practicing the various scripts can you make these skills your own.

WHAT'S COMING UP

The first three chapters of this workbook lay the groundwork for effective communication. You should read these chapters carefully and do the exercises. These are the basic skills that apply to everyone, of all ages, in all walks of life. Chapter 1 teaches listening skills, like paraphrasing, clarifying, and giving feedback, that make you more empathic toward and knowledgeable about the people who matter most to you. Chapter 2 teaches you how to open up and safely disclose important, appropriate information about yourself so that you can be known authentically by others. Chapter 3 teaches you how to express your thoughts, feelings, and desires at the right time and place to get your needs met and enhance your relationships.

The next part of this workbook teaches you communication skills that will help you cope with various types of conflict. Chapter 4 teaches you to control strong emotions, particularly anger, so that you can communicate effectively in stressful situations. Chapter 5 teaches assertiveness, the art of getting what you want without alienating others by being either too aggressive or too passive. Chapter 6 teaches fair fighting with your spouse or lover so that you can resolve conflicts fairly and quickly, improving rather than harming your relationship. Chapter 7 teaches you to negotiate good deals and fair compromises with landlords, salespeople, bosses, and bureaucrats so that you can hold your own in a competitive society. Chapter 8 teaches you how to stand up for yourself with people who have more power than you do. Chapter 9 teaches you how to talk with people who are in the throes of some painful emotion, such as fear, grief, humiliation, disappointment, or anger, so that you can help them and protect yourself at the same time.

The last part of this workbook focuses on social situations. Chapter 10 teaches you how to be sensitive and temper your messages when talking to a member of the opposite gender, so you can have a better relationship. Chapter 11 teaches you how to make contact and form relationships with new people, so you can gain a new friend or romantic partner. Chapter 12 teaches simple but effective ways to talk about sex, so you can end embarrassment and avoidance, and improve your sex life dramatically. Chapter 13 teaches you how to talk to your children so that you can gain their confidence, teach them, and keep them safe. Chapter 14 teaches you how to level with teenagers so that they hear and understand you, so you can in turn preserve your relationship with them, keep them safe, and honor their growing independence. Chapter 15 teaches the skills of communicating with elders who may have hearing, expression, or comprehension problems that make it hard to enjoy and care for them. Chapter 16 teaches you how to hold your own in a small group so that you can express your views, debate the issues, and have a positive influence in group decisions. Chapter 17 teaches the simple but essential rules of effective public speaking so that you can address an audience with maximum eloquence and minimum stage fright.

EXERCISE: DEFINE YOUR READING PLAN

Plan to read the next three chapters covering the basics. What you read after that should depend on your situation. Get off to a good start by doing the simple exercise of checking off the areas listed below that apply to you, and plan your reading accordingly. Ask yourself if you have trouble communicating

in conflict situations:

- ☐ if you have trouble containing your anger. Read chapter 4.

- ☐ when you're too passive or too aggressive. Read chapter 5.

- ☐ with your intimate partner. Read chapter 6.

- ☐ in which you have to bargain for something. Read chapter 7.

- ☐ when you are in a one-down position. Read chapter 8.

- ☐ involving highly emotional people. Read chapter 9.

in social situations:

- ☐ involving the opposite gender. Read chapter 10.

- ☐ where you might meet a new friend or lover. Read chapter 11.

with your family:

- ☐ discussing sex with your partner. Read chapter 12.

- ☐ talking with children. Read chapter 13.

- ☐ talking with teens. Read chapter 14.

- ☐ talking with elders. Read chapter 15.

in public:

- ☐ as a member of a task-oriented group. Read chapter 16.

- ☐ when you must address an audience. Read chapter 17.

Now, get started!

PART I

Laying the Groundwork for Effective Communication

CHAPTER 1

Listening: How to Really Hear What Others Have to Say

Tony, a forty-two-year-old computer salesman, was always the life of the party. He was witty, charming, had a collection of funny anecdotes about his clientele, and didn't mind making a fool of himself in the telling. He regularly turned up at parties with a pretty woman by his side. It was a different pretty woman each time. Somehow, Tony couldn't seem to keep any of them interested long enough to develop a serious, intimate relationship. At work, the situation wasn't much better. Although his sales figures were good enough, Tony was by no means one of the top sellers, and his bonuses were few and far between. Recently, he'd asked one of his girlfriends why she didn't want to go out with him anymore, and she'd told him that he didn't seem terribly interested in her. Flabbergasted, he questioned her further. "You're a nice guy, Tony," she said. "But you never listen to anyone but yourself."

There are many benefits to good listening. The more you really hear what others are expressing, the better you can understand other people and their needs. The better you understand their needs, the more you can choose to facilitate those needs being met. A genuine desire to understand the people in your life leads to increased intimacy while encouraging others (by example) to try to listen to and understand you. The result is that your relationships will significantly improve. In the workplace, listening better to colleagues, people whom you supervise as well as those above you, will not only improve morale but may reap more tangible rewards as you become better equipped to meet the company's needs.

REAL LISTENING VERSUS PSEUDO LISTENING

It's hard to really listen, though everyone assumes that they do. And of course you do listen, to some extent. You hear your boss tell you that the general meeting has been postponed. You hear your friend tell you what time the party is on Saturday night. You hear your partner tell you that he or she is going to bed. You may even think of yourself as a good listener. But are you? Real listening is difficult—and much more rare—than many people realize.

Real listening is more than just being quiet while the other person talks. It's more than being able to parrot back what the other person says, as if your brain were a tape recorder. Real listening implies that you want to understand what the other person is saying and, therefore, what that person thinks, feels, and needs. It means putting aside your own ideas and judgments long enough to really hear. This takes effort. It's easier to listen with only a part of your consciousness while the other part rehearses your own story, develops a brilliant retort, or tunes out because you've "heard it before."

Pseudo listening gives the appearance of real listening. Everyone does it at least some of the time. Pseudo listening serves needs that differ from those involved in real listening. You may want to consider which of those needs might be interfering with your ability to really listen. Try to honestly evaluate your motivations when talking with the important people in your life. Examine how your particular needs interfere with your ability to listen. To whom do you have the hardest time really listening? Do you always have difficulty listening to this person or only when you are conversing about certain topics? Do the circumstances in which you are talking sometimes alter your motivation, along with your ability to really listen?

Bronwyn spent almost two weeks gathering information about what motivated her to use pseudo listening with the important people in her life. She used the following worksheets to reword her discoveries.

Motivation	At Work				At Home	
	Boss	Colleague	Subordinate	Client	Spouse/ Partner	Children
Wanting to be liked		X				
Checking for signs of rejection		X				
Hunting for a specific piece of information						
Preparing your response	X					
Listening so you'll be listened to						
Listening for weak points; gathering ammunition						
Checking if you've achieved the right effect	X				X	
Trying to be "good" or "nice"						
Not knowing how to leave without offending						
Other						

Bronwyn's Motivations for Pseudo Listening at Work and Home

Bronwyn's Motivations for Pseudo Listening with Friends and Relatives

Motivation	With Friends			With Relatives			
	Best	Same sex	Opposite sex	Mom	Dad	Siblings	Other
Wanting to be liked	X	X	X				
Checking for signs of rejection						X	
Hunting for a specific piece of information							
Preparing your response				X	X	X	
Listening so you'll be listened to							
Listening for weak points; gathering ammunition							
Checking if you've achieved the right effect		X	X				
Trying to be "good" or "nice"							
Not knowing how to leave without offending							
Other							

Bronwyn discovered that she tended to have the hardest time listening to authority figures: her boss, her parents, and her older sister. Her motivation for pseudo listening tended to reflect her early experiences of feeling criticized. Regardless of the situation or topic being discussed, Bronwyn spent her time with these people preparing her response. With colleagues (she had no subordinates or clients), her boyfriend, and other friends, the motivations for pseudo listening included wanting to be liked, checking for signs of rejection, and checking to make sure she was producing the right effect. Only with her best friend, Nancy, did she feel able to really listen, and even then, real listening gave way to her strong desire to be liked whenever the topic focused on Nancy's other friends.

Over the next few days or weeks, fill out these two worksheets to see what you can learn about yourself.

Motivation	At Work				At Home	
	Boss	Colleague	Subordinate	Client	Spouse/ Partner	Children
Your Motivations for Pseudo Listening at Work and Home						
Wanting to be liked						
Checking for signs of rejection						
Hunting for a specific piece of information						
Preparing your response						
Listening so you'll be listened to						
Listening for weak points; gathering ammunition						
Checking if you've achieved the right effect						
Trying to be "good" or "nice"						
Not knowing how to leave without offending						
Other						

Your Motivations for Pseudo Listening with Friends and Relatives							
Motivation	With Friends			With Relatives			
	Best	Same sex	Opposite sex	Mom	Dad	Siblings	Other
Wanting to be liked							
Checking for signs of rejection							
Hunting for a specific piece of information							
Preparing your response							
Listening so you'll be listened to							
Listening for weak points; gathering ammunition							
Checking if you've achieved the right effect							
Trying to be "good" or "nice"							
Not knowing how to leave without offending							
Other							

BLOCKS TO LISTENING

There are twelve common blocks to listening. As you read through this list, you'll probably notice that some listening blocks resonate with a familiarity bred of regular use. Others may seem less relevant. The twelve blocks are:

- comparing

- mind reading

- rehearsing

- filtering

- judging

- dreaming

- identifying

- advising

- sparring

- being right

- derailing

- placating

Comparing

It's hard to really listen when you're constantly comparing yourself to the other person, checking to see if you measure up in terms of intelligence, wit, emotional stability, competence, or even level of suffering. For example, at every family gathering, Cathy found herself comparing her successes and accomplishments with those of her two older sisters. She even compared their children's achievements with her children's achievements.

Mind Reading

If you pay more attention to what you think someone "really means" (based primarily on your own feelings, assumptions, or hunches) than to what he or she is actually saying, then you are mind reading. For instance, when Peggy told her husband that she was too tired to go to the ball game and preferred instead to stay home and watch a video, he "knew that she really meant" that she was angry and was punishing him.

Rehearsing

Rehearsing occurs when you mentally plan your response to what someone is saying to you while the other person is still speaking. This keeps you from really listening. For example, when Mariano was telling his mother why he wanted to go with his friends to the concert, instead of listening she was running through all the reasons she couldn't afford the ticket.

Filtering

When you filter, you may tune out certain topics or you may hear only certain things and tune everything else out. For instance, in conversations with her boyfriend, Amanda used filtering to listen for—and react to—any possible hint of unhappiness, no matter what he actually said. Her boyfriend, on the other hand, filtered out anything Amanda said that had to do with her ex-husband.

Judging

You are judging if you decide ahead of time that the other person is not worth hearing (because he or she is "stupid," "crazy," "hypocritical," or " immature"), and that you will therefore listen only in order to confirm your opinion. For example, Lester thought that his sales partner was a loser and listened only to the things his partner said that supported that judgment.

Dreaming

When you're dreaming, you pay only a fraction of your attention to the person talking; inside, your thoughts are wandering elsewhere. For instance, while Ian was telling his best friend, Patrick, about his latest romantic conquest, Patrick suddenly found himself thinking about the weekend he'd just spent in Mendocino with his wife.

Identifying

You are identifying when whatever you hear from the other person triggers memories of your own similar experiences, and you can't wait to launch into your own story. Linda was telling her colleague Marjorie about a negative interaction she'd just had with their boss. "He did that to me, just last week," interrupted Marjorie, "and it was even more humiliating because the CEO was listening!"

Advising

Jumping in with advice when the other person has barely stopped talking (or before) is a sign that you are advising rather than listening. Fixing things may not even be what the other person wants. For example, when Cherie was telling her cousin how she felt hurt by the man she was dating, her cousin couldn't wait until Cherie finished talking to start giving advice: "You shouldn't let him do that to you.

Just tell him to bug off. When he calls to ask you out again, tell him you're too busy. Or better yet, let the answering machine answer the call, and then don't call him back."

Sparring

If you listen only long enough to find something to disagree with, and then assert your position—regardless of what the other person says—you are sparring. Sparring can include sarcasm and put-downs. For instance, when John was explaining why he wasn't enjoying being on the basketball team anymore, his coach started pointing out all the flaws in his reasoning. It didn't matter what John said. His coach had a conflicting opinion about it.

Being Right

If you go to great lengths to prove that you're right or to avoid the suggestion that you're wrong—including lying, shouting, twisting the facts, changing the subject, making excuses, and accusing—then you're not listening. For example, when ten-year-old Tonja said she thought it was mean of her mom not to let her watch the end of the movie, her mother responded, "That's not mean. Besides, you already watched most of it. Anyway, you're obviously cranky today, so I probably shouldn't even have let you stay up and watch as much as you did."

Derailing

You're guilty of derailing if you change the subject or make a joke whenever you become bored or uncomfortable with the conversation. For instance, every time Carlos began expressing his concerns to his wife about the expenses she incurred, she laughed it off or started talking about something else.

Placating

If you're so concerned with being nice, agreeable, or liked that without really listening you agree with everything being said, you are placating. Ivory was helping his younger sister, Linda, with a science project. Linda was so happy with Ivory's attention, she agreed with whatever he suggested, whether or not it fit the project description.

EXERCISE: IDENTIFYING LISTENING BLOCKS

To make sure that you understand the twelve listening blocks described above, read the following vignettes and identify the blocks that were used by each person.

Vignette 1: It was Friday evening, and Bradley and Tyler were having a few drinks after work. They weren't exactly friends; in fact, Tyler supposed that Bradley was a bit of a buffoon. But because they had adjacent offices and both were recently divorced, they felt like they should have something in common. Bradley leaned against the bar. "So, what are your plans for the weekend?" he asked Tyler. "Not much," Tyler replied. He thought wistfully of the picnics he and Amy used to have by the lake. "You should get out, meet some girls, have yourself a good time," said Bradley. "Be good for you." "Nah," sighed Tyler. "Not this weekend. I'm not feeling much like kicking up my heels right now." "But that's just it," said Bradley, "You have to push yourself. Believe me, I know what I'm talking about. If you let yourself stay at home and mope, then she's won. Besides, there's a great party over at Steve's on Saturday." As Bradley described the party's attractions, and the reasons why Tyler should come, Tyler found his own thoughts wandering. "I guess Bradley thinks I'm failing at coping with Divorce 101," he thought to himself. "Well, maybe I am. I'm sure not coping as well as he is. He seems to be doing just fine. But hell, he's also such a jerk. Why doesn't he just shut up?" He thought about the way he and Amy would exchange glances, and how Amy would roll her eyes when someone was especially long-winded. "So, what do you think?" asked Bradley. Tyler pulled his attention back to the conversation. He realized he didn't know what Bradley was asking. "I don't know" was the safest answer he could think of. "Well I do," stated Bradley. "And I think you should definitely come. I'll even pick you up on my way." "He's like a damned bulldog," thought Tyler, "just won't let go. He must really think I'm a basket case."

In the space below, write the listening blocks that Bradley and Tyler demonstrated.

Bradley's listening blocks: _____

_____

Tyler's listening blocks: _____

_____

Vignette 2: Dinner was long over, the kids were in bed, and Chinelo and Damien were reviewing their day. They'd already talked about Damien's ongoing conflict with his boss, and Chinelo's potential promotion. "Mom called and asked if next month is okay for a visit," Damien said, a little anxiously. He knew this wasn't an easy topic for them. "Oh, I almost forgot!" exclaimed Chinelo. "Justin has a soccer tournament this weekend. You're going to have to deal with the carpool again." "I knew she wouldn't want Mom to visit," Damien thought to himself. "I'm sure she thinks I invited her down just to yank her chain. I'd better tread lightly about this soccer thing and maybe she'll realize I'm not trying to cause trouble. Though heaven knows carting around a carload of soccer boys is the last thing I was hoping to do this weekend." To Chinelo, he said, "No problem with the soccer details. Just leave them to me." "Fine," replied Chinelo. Damien took a deep breath, "So, what do you think about Mom's—," he began. "Don't forget you also agreed to write that letter to the zoning board before next Monday," Chinelo interrupted. "I won't forget, sweetheart," replied Damien, and as Chinelo continued expressing her thoughts aloud on the zoning issues, he continued thinking, "Now what do I say? Chinelo's giving me the 'no' loud and clear, and if I push harder, she'll really get mad. But if I don't get it settled, I'll get no end of guff from Mom." He thought of using his Mom's visit as an opportunity for some free babysitting, but rejected that approach, and couldn't think of another. He gave up for the evening. "I'm tired, sweetheart," he said heavily, "I'm going to hit the sack."

In the space below, write the listening blocks that Chinelo and Damien demonstrated.

Chinelo: _____

_____

Damien: _____

_____

Vignette 3: Kathleen, Lisa, and Heather had gathered at Lisa's kitchen table in her new apartment. Heather was silently appraising the place, comparing it with her own. Though slightly smaller, her own apartment was nevertheless more attractive, she concluded, definitely the result of her more sophisticated taste. She was startled when Kathleen poked her in the ribs saying, "Hey, wake up! Coffee or tea?" "Oh, tea," she replied. "Decaf please." "Sorry," apologized Lisa. "Only regular Lipton's at this point. I haven't had time for a real grocery run." Heather almost raised an eyebrow but caught herself. "More sophisticated *and* more organized," she said to herself, feeling rather pleased. "Fine," she said aloud, and turned her thoughts to her own housewarming party, which had been a huge success. Meanwhile, Kathleen and Lisa were chatting about the night class in multimedia networking that the three of them were enrolled in. Lisa had missed the last two classes, and Kathleen was a little worried that she might be considering dropping out. "With work and getting organized here, I'm exhausted at night," Lisa said. "We're doing some really fun applications this week," encouraged Kathleen. "You really should come." "I think the photography class I did last year was the most fun," said Lisa. "But of course I was dating that cute guy who was the teaching assistant." "Mollie—you know, with the hennaed hair—has suggested that we all go out after class this week for drinks; maybe even dinner," said Kathleen. "We used to go to the Cock and Crow every week after photography," reminisced Lisa. "It was a real hoot. Sometimes we'd stay till closing without realizing. It was an incredibly stimulating group. I don't even remember what we'd talk about, but we'd go on and on for hours."

In the space below, write the listening blocks that Heather, Lisa, and Kathleen demonstrated.

Heather: _____

_____

Lisa: _____

_____

Kathleen: _____

_____

Check your answers:

In vignette 1, Bradley wasn't really interested in what Tyler was saying or what he was feeling. He was too busy *advising*, *sparring*, and *being right*. Tyler, on the other hand, was prevented from listening by his *comparing*, *mind reading*, *judging*, and *dreaming*.

In vignette 2, Chinelo used *filtering* every time Damien began talking about his mother and used *derailing* to change the topic. Damien's blocks to listening included *mind reading*, *placating*, and *rehearsing*.

In vignette 3, Heather was more interested in *comparing* and *dreaming* than in really listening. Lisa's main block was her tendency to *identify*, while Kathleen *filtered* out any suggestion that Lisa wasn't committed to the class.

Now that you've practiced identifying the twelve listening blocks, take a few minutes to think about which blocks tend to prevent you from really listening at work, at home, with friends, and with relatives. Write them in the spaces below:

At work (with boss, colleagues, subordinates, clients): _____

_____

_____

At home (with spouse/partner, children): _____

_____

_____

With friends (best friend, same-sex friends, opposite-sex friends): _____

_____

_____

With relatives (parents, siblings, others): _____

_____

_____

EXERCISE: WHAT IS LISTENING?

Think about an occasion in your past when you tried unsuccessfully to tell someone (a partner, friend, parent, colleague, or someone else) something important. Answer the questions in the space provided.

What was the other person's response? _____

_____

_____

Did that response make you want to continue talking, saying more about your feelings or thoughts? Or were you frustrated, disappointed, or angry? _____

_____

_____

What blocks to listening did the other person use? _____

_____

Is this a fairly consistent pattern of response from that person? _____

How did the other person's response make you feel about your relationship? About yourself and the things you had to say? _____

_____

_____

Is there someone in your life who really listens to what you have to say? What does that person do that makes you feel good? _____

_____

_____

EXERCISE: PRACTICING YOUR RESPONSE

Consider this situation: You're at your company picnic, feasting on scorched hot dogs and slightly under-cooked potato salad. The colleagues you've been chatting with move away to refill their glasses. A casual friend wanders over and says hello. You like this person and have tried to encourage the friendship, so you nod to the chair next to you and your friend sits down. "I know this probably isn't the time or place to talk about this," she begins, "but I really need some help." You've barely nodded before your friend starts pouring out the story: "It's my son, my fifteen-year-old. I think he's using drugs. Last night, when he came home, he seemed spacey and his pupils were really dilated. And it's not the first time I've thought that. But when I asked him about it, he got really angry, started swearing at me, and actually shoved me against the wall as he went past. Now I'm scared to raise it with him again. He's strong and I don't feel safe. But I'm scared to ignore it too. I don't know what to do."

You want to be helpful. Without thinking further about it, write down what you would say to your friend: _____

_____

_____

_____

Now think about the person you described earlier, the person who really listens to you and makes you feel good. What would he or she say to your friend? Using that person as a guide, write down the most helpful response you can think of: _____

_____

_____

Compare the two responses. Is there a difference? If so, which do you think would feel the more helpful or supportive? Was the second response more helpful? Was your initial, automatic response similar to the kind of responses you have received in the past, either as a child or more recently?

Because it's familiar, your first response may be automatic, even when you know from your own experience that it's not really helpful. On the other hand, even when you know what it's like to feel really listened to, you may not know exactly how to do it for someone else.

LISTENING SKILLS

There are three major rules to observe when you want someone to feel really heard: listen with full attention; listen for the feelings as well as the content; actively acknowledge what you've heard.

Listen with Full Attention

This is probably the hardest of the three rules to observe because it really requires *full* attention. Unlike pseudo listening, it requires the desire to hear and understand. That means putting down the newspaper or book you're in the middle of or closing the magazine you've been leafing through. It means turning off the TV or the computer game you're enjoying. Full attention also means suspending your judgment about what the other person is saying, not minimizing, criticizing, analyzing, or trying to solve the problems presented.

Part of paying attention is *showing* with your body that you're listening. Maintain eye contact, nod, lean slightly forward, and smile or frown in accordance with what is being said.

Listen for the Feelings As Well As the Content

Attending to the feelings as well as the content of the message may take some practice. It's important to remember that listening to and acknowledging someone's feelings doesn't mean agreeing with those feelings, nor does it mean sharing them. It does mean being aware of them, which takes *empathy*, the ability to put yourself in the other person's shoes and understand his or her feelings. Fine-tuning your awareness means paying attention to the other person's body language. Facial expressions, tone of voice, body posture, and so forth can give you important information. Try to imagine how you might feel under similar circumstances.

When you first start practicing listening skills, you might want to use the four major feeling categories—glad, mad, sad, and bad—to help you understand how someone else feels. *Glad* contains all the positive feelings (happy, confident, proud, cheerful, delighted, and so forth). *Mad* includes such feelings as angry, resentful, annoyed, furious, and frustrated. *Sad* describes such feelings as disappointed, gloomy, troubled, miserable, upset, and despairing. *Bad* includes any feelings that don't fit in the other categories: afraid, bored, confused, desperate, embarrassed, guilty, helpless, panicky, worried, and so on.

Once you identify which of the four main categories the person's feelings fit into, it might help to run through a bigger list of fairly typical feelings to identify his or her feelings more closely. Use the following list as a guide.

Glad	Mad	Sad	Bad
amused	angry	defeated	afraid
cheerful	annoyed	dejected	anxious
confident	enraged	depressed	bored
delighted	frustrated	despairing	confused
excited	furious	disappointed	desperate
grateful	impatient	discouraged	embarrassed
happy	irked	gloomy	guilty
pleased	irritated	hopeless	helpless
proud	livid	lonely	horrified
relieved	resentful	miserable	isolated
satisfied	violated	pessimistic	needy
secure		resigned	overwhelmed
thrilled		troubled	panicky
		unappreciated	pressured
		unfulfilled	stuck
		unloved	threatened
		upset	trapped
		vulnerable	uneasy
			worried

Actively Acknowledge What You've Heard

This is the final rule for listening. Acknowledging doesn't mean agreeing, and it doesn't preclude placing limits on the other person's behavior (it might be okay for the person to be angry but not okay for him or her to yell at you or to punch holes in the wall). Acknowledging means letting the other person know in some verbal way that you've heard what's been said to you, both the content and the feelings.

It's difficult to acknowledge painful or angry feelings. The key is to respect the other person's right to his or her own opinion and feelings even when you may disagree with them. Acknowledgment can range from a simple expression such as "What a nightmare!" to more complex statements that include the content and feelings expressed by the other person. For example, "You sound really worried about Tim and the decisions he's facing," or "Boy! I can imagine how helpless you must feel in the wake of getting that news," or "Sounds like you're feeling really hopeless about things getting resolved with your wife."

There are three ways to actively acknowledge that you've heard someone: paraphrasing, or putting into your own words what you heard; clarifying any information that wasn't completely clear; and giving feedback.

Paraphrasing

For simple interactions, simple responses work the best. But for more important interactions, when it's important to you that the other person really feels heard and acknowledged, you should paraphrase what he or she has said. Paraphrasing means saying in your own words what you've just heard. For example, "It sounds like you're really ashamed of the way you reacted to Tara's refusal. Almost as if pleading with her made you less of a man."

Clarifying

Sometimes you may really listen to what's being said, and yet you're still not totally clear about what the other person is feeling or meaning. Under those circumstances, it's important to ask for clarification. Respect doesn't mean understanding everything all the time, but it does mean *wanting* to understand, which sometimes requires asking questions. Ask specific questions. "You sound upset, but I'm not totally clear what part of this is upsetting to you" is more likely to yield clarifying information than "I don't get it."

Giving Feedback

Once you've listened to and understood what the other person has said, it may be time to give that person some feedback. Giving feedback means telling the other person your reaction to what he or she has said. Feedback must be immediate, honest, and supportive. *Immediate* means that you give your response as soon as possible without delay. *Honest* means that you give your true reaction, revealing your own feelings, without fear of offending. *Supportive* means stating your honest reaction in ways that are tolerable to hear rather than deliberately hurtful or brutal. "I'm disappointed that you didn't consult with me before making that decision" is more supportive than "that was really stupid and irresponsible of you."

EXERCISE: GENERAL LISTENING PRACTICE

With each of the important people in your life, you can make a conscious decision to practice really listening for fifteen minutes a day. Use the chart below to monitor your progress. Choose someone and write down his or her name in each category that applies to you. For each person, rate yourself on your ability to demonstrate each of the three listening skills. Use a scale of 0 to 10, where 0 means you are not really listening at all, and 10 means you are deftly using all three skills. Continue practicing on successive days until you are able to award yourself high marks for each skill. Make as many copies of the chart as you think you'll need.

Important people (Select those who apply)	Listen with full attention (rate yourself 0 to 10)	Listen for feelings as well as content (rate yourself 0 to 10)	Actively acknowledge what you heard (rate yourself 0 to 10)
Boss:			
Colleague:			
Subordinate:			
Client:			
Spouse/partner:			
Children:			
Best friend:			
Same-sex friend:			
Opposite-sex friend:			
Mom:			
Dad:			
Siblings:			
Other relative:			

EXERCISE: WORKING ON RECIPROCAL COMMUNICATION

This is an exercise to do with your spouse or partner or a close friend. Pick a topic that is of concern to both of you but not more than a mild source of conflict. Discuss the topic, taking turns being the speaker and the listener. When you're the speaker, remember to express your views and feelings succinctly and without blame.

Stop after two or three minutes and let your listening partner summarize what you've said. If your partner is having difficulty paraphrasing (summarizing) what you've said, try to speak even more succinctly. Answer any clarifying questions. When your partner has finished, point out anything that's been left out.

When you're the listener, remember to pay close attention and listen to the other person's feelings as well as the content of what he or she is saying. Don't argue or interrupt, and ask questions only to clarify what you don't understand. Continue clarifying and summarizing until your partner feels completely heard and understood. Then switch places and do the exercise again, choosing a new topic.

Miki and Christian did the first part of the exercise in the following way, with Miki speaking and Christian listening:

Miki: I'm concerned about the kids not getting to bed on time. We agreed that they should go to bed at eight and it seems like often the light's not out until almost nine, especially on the nights when I'm at work. Sometimes when I've called at nine, they're still up! When they've had a late night, they have a harder time getting up in the morning, and it seems like they're cranky when they do get up. That makes getting them ready for school harder, and I end up having to yell at them to get them out the door on time. I hate starting the day off like that, especially when I've worked the night before and this is my first contact with them.

Christian: Okay, so you hate starting the day yelling at the kids, especially when you've been working and haven't seen them, and you think I should put them to bed earlier.

Miki: Yes, but you forgot why I think they need their sleep.

Christian: Right. You think when they go to bed late, they don't get up as easily and don't get ready for school on time.

Miki: And they're cranky.

Christian: And they're cranky.

Miki: Right.

Miki and Christian swapped roles, and Christian took the role of speaker. This time, pay close attention to what Christian says, and then put yourself in Miki's role and write your own summary of what he said.

Christian: Well, when you're at work, I'm on my own with the kids. I don't get to pick them up until almost six. It's almost seven before I get dinner made. Then they always want to have a bath, and sometimes there's homework that hasn't been done, and I want them to have a little time for playing. Then it's eight thirty and time for them to get into bed and read a little. I've worked all day and I'm exhausted too. I don't feel like rushing them, and I'm not willing to yell at them either.

Your summary: _____

_____

_____

_____

Repeated practice of this exercise will help you in all areas of your life. Try and do it on a daily basis. It just takes a few minutes, but the rewards are incalculable.

CHAPTER 2

Opening Up: When, What, and to Whom to Disclose about Yourself

Self-disclosure is the revealing of personal facts, feelings, and opinions to others. It can be as simple and easy as revealing your birthday to a fellow astrology buff or as complex and scary as sharing sexual fantasies with a new lover.

Self-disclosure is not really optional. You can't help disclosing things about yourself. Even if you ignore those around you, your silence communicates itself to them. Your clothes, grooming, posture, and gestures say something about you before you even open your mouth to speak.

Revealing yourself is often difficult. You may hold back because others might disapprove of you or disagree with your most cherished beliefs. Someone might laugh or leave or say no. Sometimes it doesn't feel appropriate to talk a lot about yourself, to toot your own horn, or to monopolize the conversation.

HOW SELF-DISCLOSURE CAN BENEFIT YOU

Since the 1950s, researchers and humanist psychologists have suggested that people who disclose more about themselves tend to be happier, more confident, and more successful. They enjoy self-disclosure's five key benefits:

- **Reciprocal communication.** Disclosure breeds disclosure. As you open up to others, they in turn open up to you. Communication improves because there are more personal and significant topics on the table. What you say and what is said to you is more interesting, more profound, and more satisfying to reveal and hear.

- **Increased self-knowledge and self-esteem.** As you explain yourself to others, you grow in self-knowledge. The process of putting your thoughts, fears, and feelings into words sharpens your internal picture of yourself. What has been vague and contradictory becomes more sharply defined and delineated. As you know yourself better, you tend to like or esteem yourself more.

- **Deeper intimacy.** When partners in a close relationship withhold large parts of themselves, the relationship is shallow and unsatisfying. As you reveal more and more of yourself, your partner opens up as well, and you both reap the benefits of a more intense, satisfying relationship.

- **Increased energy.** Nothing is more deadening than a secret that weighs on your mind. It takes energy to withhold important information about yourself. When you are harboring a secret from those around you, you feel tired and stressed all the time. When you finally reveal the secret, a great psychic load is lifted from your spirit and you feel a rush of relief and renewed energy.

- **Relief from guilt and shame.** Disclosure can relieve guilt by lifting the burden of secrecy. Revealing something of which you are ashamed is a spiritual experience of confession and often absolution as well. Others are rarely as harsh in their judgments as you have been in the court of your own mind. They are usually more inclined to forgive you than you are to forgive yourself.

A WINDOW ON YOUR SELF

In 1954, University of California personality researchers Joseph Luft and Harry Ingham invented the "Johari Window," named by combining letters from their names. The Johari Window is a graphic representation of your self as it is known to you and to others:

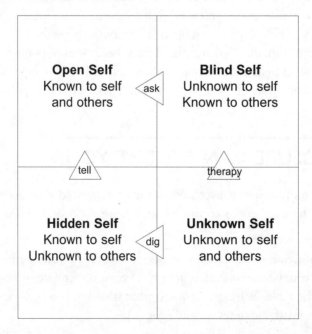

These four boxes represent all that can be known about you. Your Open Self contains all the information that you reveal to others, such as your appearance, age, gender, name, and so on. Your Hidden Self contains all that you know about yourself and choose not to reveal, such as your worst fears, misdeeds, obsessions, and so on. Your Blind Self contains all that is obvious to others but unknown by you, such as your bad breath or rapid blinking when you're nervous. The Unknown Self contains everything that neither you nor others are aware of, such as forgotten childhood experiences or repressed memories of trauma.

The arrows indicate how information moves from one part of your self-awareness to another. Self-disclosure is the process of making your Open Self larger by telling others about your Hidden Self. When you ask others for feedback, you are moving information about yourself from your Blind Self to your Open Self. When you practice introspection, meditation, dream analysis, journaling, or stream-of-consciousness writing, you dig information about yourself out of your Unknown Self. Then again, if you undergo therapy with a very perceptive therapist, there may be times when he or she deduces something about you that resides in your Unknown Self, moving it into your Blind Self— known to him or her but not yet known to you.

HOW MUCH DO YOU DISCLOSE?

Some people are more forthcoming than others. Wendy was an extrovert who found it easy to talk to anyone about herself. Her Open Self was relatively large. The sizes of her various selves can best be seen in a pie chart you could call the "Johari porthole."

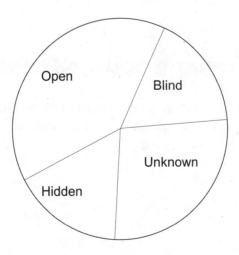

Wendy talking to Sally

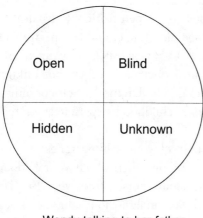

Wendy talking to her father

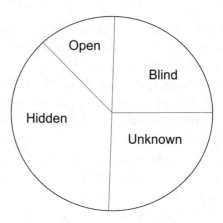

Wendy talking to her caseworker

Actually, your Johari profile changes constantly, depending on whom you're talking to. The window on the previous page represents Wendy talking freely and openly with her best friend, Sally. Compare it to the windows below.

Notice how the size of Wendy's Open Self contracts when she is talking with her father and shrinks even more dramatically when she is talking to her caseworker about her eligibility for disability. Not only does she keep more hidden when she's talking to authority figures, but she also can see less of her Blind Self, since she is unlikely to ask for feedback or really hear it when she receives it.

In the normal course of a day, you choose to reveal or hide more of yourself, depending on your audience and the situations in which you find yourself. The next exercise will give you a chance to discover how open you are and how you close up or reveal more with different people.

EXERCISE: WHAT IS YOUR JOHARI WINDOW?

In general, are you a relatively open person or a closed person? Draw your average Johari window here, showing the relative sizes of your Open, Hidden, Blind, and Unknown selves.

Next, think about how you disclose yourself to important people in your life. For each topic on the left in the chart below, think about how you have talked with your parents, siblings, children, best friends, and spouse or partner. If your parents are dead or you currently have no partner, change the headings to someone else in your life, or ignore those categories.

Rate how much you reveal about each topic to each important person in your life. Fill in the blanks using a scale of 0 to 3, in which

0 means you've revealed *nothing* about this.

1 means you've revealed *part* of the facts about this.

2 means you've revealed *everything* about this.

3 means you've *lied* about this.

How Much Do You Reveal about Yourself to These Important People?						
Your tastes in	Mom	Dad	Siblings	Spouse/ Partner	Children	Same-sex Friend	Opposite-sex Friend
Food							
Music							
Fashion							
Books and magazines							
Movies and TV shows							
Web sites							
Houses and furnishings							
Parties or other social gatherings							
Other _____							
Your opinions about							
Politics							
Religion							
Race							
Drugs and Alcohol							
Sex							

Your tastes in	Mom	Dad	Siblings	Spouse/ Partner	Children	Same-sex Friend	Opposite-sex Friend
What's attractive in a man							
What's attractive in a woman							
Other _____							
Your work or studies							
Your strong points							
What you enjoy most							
Your weaknesses							
What you enjoy least							
Relationship with bosses or teachers							
Relationship with peers							
Goals							
Other _____							
Your money							
How much you make or receive							
Sources of income							
Debts							
Savings							
What others owe you							
Gambling							
Bad habits							
Other _____							
Your personality							
Virtues—what you like about yourself							

Vices—what you don't like							
Feelings you hide							
Feelings you can't control							
Other _____							
Your sex life							
With whom							
What you like							
What you don't like							
What you're ashamed of, regret, feel guilty about							
What you fear most							
Favorite fantasy							
Other _____							
Your body							
Medical history							
Current health problems							
How you keep fit or don't							
How you'd like to look							
How you feel about your body: face, waist, feet, and so on							
Other _____							

Notice which topics are easier for you to talk about—the ones rated with a 1 or a 2. Who are you the most open with? With whom are you more reserved? Which topics do you find difficult to share, whoever the audience is?

When Evie did this exercise, she noticed that she had little trouble talking to her friends about music and fashion. She could talk to her mom about politics or her dad about painful feelings, but not vice versa. She didn't want to tell anyone, even her boyfriend, about her sex life or how she felt about certain areas of her body. She had actively lied about or evaded questions about how much she owed on her credit cards.

EXERCISE: OPENING THE WINDOW

How much of yourself do you want to disclose to different people? This exercise will help you decide what you need to reveal and to whom. Look back over the previous exercise and examine the topics and people you rated with 0s and 3s. Whom have you been keeping in the dark? To whom do you lie? Among the important people in your life, one or two will stand out as people from whom you are keeping a secret about yourself.

Use this information to determine what you need to say and to whom you need to say it. Then fill in the blanks below.

1. "I need to tell _____ about _____ ."

2. "I need to tell _____ about _____ ."

3. "I need to tell _____ about _____ ."

4. "I need to tell _____ about _____ ."

Evie realized that it was ridiculous for her to be withholding information about her politics from her dad. She also noticed a connection between her withholding information about the extent of her credit card debt and the trouble she and her boyfriend Bill had been having discussing anything about their future. Here's how Evie filled in the blanks:

1. "I need to tell _____Dad_____ about _____my politics_____ ."

2. "I need to tell _____Bill_____ about _____my credit card debt_____ ."

EXERCISE: PRACTICE SELF-DISCLOSURE IN STAGES

Deciding to tell is one thing. Actually doing it is another. It helps to disclose in stages, starting with the least threatening material.

It's easier to talk about facts than it is to talk about deeply held beliefs or strong feelings. It's also easier to talk about what's past and gone than about what's here and now. Try breaking your disclosure into the following stages and revealing information to the important people in your life over two or more conversations.

1. The facts in the past: _____

2. Your thoughts and feelings in the past: _____

3. The facts here and now: _____

4. Your thoughts and feelings here and now: _____

It may help you to jot down the information before trying to talk about it. Here's how Evie broke up what she had to say about her credit card debt:

1. The facts in the past: *I grew up poor, and had to wait forever to get a toy or a new dress.*

2. My thoughts and feelings in the past: *I felt deprived and thought good things were scarce in the world.*

3. The facts here and now: *I now have three maxed-out credit cards on which I owe over $9,000.*

4. My thoughts and feelings here and now: *I feel stupid and out of control. Embarrassed that I'm still acting like a teenager who wants a new dress.*

One day when they were out shopping in a huge discount store, Evie told Bill about her childhood poverty and view of the universe as a realm of scarcity. A few days later, she came clean about her debts and feelings in the here and now. She confided that she was afraid Bill would never want to make a long-term commitment to her because she was such a liability financially. Bill assured her that money was not the basis of their relationship and offered to do anything he could to support her in getting out of debt.

It was more difficult for Evie to disclose her political ideals to her conservative father. She started by writing down these four stages of disclosure:

1. The facts in the past: *In my heart, I've always preferred Democrats to Republicans.*

2. My feelings in the past: *I was too overwhelmed by the strength of Dad's conservatism to speak up about politics.*

3. The facts here and now: *I'm more radicalized now. I'd call myself almost a libertarian on some questions and am a Green Party sympathizer on environmental issues.*

4. My feelings here and now: *I'm ashamed to not be able to speak up, but am still somewhat afraid. I want my Dad to know where I stand, even if it's opposed to his ideas, even if it's scary.*

Evie blurted out her past facts and feelings during a lunch with her Dad and Mom. She knew that her Mom would keep things civil. Later she talked with her Dad in private about her timidity around him. It was easier than she thought it would be. They began to have some lively political debates, and she was proud to be able to express her true views and defend them.

Evie's relationship with Bill blossomed as she began to disclose more important information about herself. Bill started to open up as well, telling her more about his past and his feelings about things now. Their conversations became deeper and more interesting. They felt closer than ever, with less boredom, less friction, and less doubt about their compatibility. Evie liked herself more and felt less guilty and bogged down by unrevealed feelings.

START SLOWLY, BUT START

When you begin to disclose tender information about yourself, don't start with the most personal subject or the most judgmental audience. Pick a more neutral topic and a person who you know will treat you gently. Start with pure information, just the historical facts. Gradually include what is going on in the here and now, including your current feelings. When you have had success disclosing safe information about yourself to a safe person, then try it with a more difficult topic or person.

CHAPTER 3

Expressing Yourself: Creating Clear and Effective Messages

Expressing yourself clearly and effectively reaps these rewards:

- mutual understanding

- cooperation from others

- getting your needs met

- enhanced intimacy

The following conversation between Jenny and Mike illustrates what happens when communication is neither clear nor effective. It's Saturday afternoon, and Jenny and Mike are driving to the grocery store to do their weekly shopping. They both work long hours during the week, so this is one of the few times they have to talk.

Jenny: Would you like to have lunch at Pepe's?

Mike: No. I want to get back and mow the lawn.

Jenny: You can do that later.

Mike: No. I also have to clean the roof and the gutters, and I promised I'd help Steve with his computer.

Jenny: Well, aren't you the busy little beaver? You never have time for us anymore. All you think about is work, work, work!

Mike: (raising his voice) That's not fair. I'm doing this for us, and Steve really needs my help! He does a lot for us. I want to return the favor. You're always nagging me about something.

Jenny: (whining) All I was asking for was a little time alone with you. For your information, I'm starving! We haven't eaten in seven hours. You're always making such a big deal out of things!

As you can see, any possibility for a pleasant time together is extinguished, and both Jenny and Mike end up feeling like victims, unfairly attacked by the other. If Jenny had expressed herself more clearly from the beginning, Mike would have understood her point of view and would have not become defensive.

WHOLE MESSAGES VS. PARTIAL MESSAGES

The people who are important to you can only understand you and know if it makes sense to cooperate with you when you share your experiences in a straightforward way. This means giving accurate feedback about what you observe, clearly stating your opinion, revealing your feelings, and letting people know what you want. In this chapter, you will learn to express *whole messages* that include these four elements:

- Observations: You report only what your senses tell you.

- Opinions: You draw conclusions, based on what you have heard, read and observed, about what is really going on and why. You make value judgments about what is good and bad.

- Feelings: You give your emotional response to an event.

- Needs: You express what you want or think you must have in a given situation.

In contrast to whole messages, *partial messages* leave out one or more of the above four elements. Partial messages can create unnecessary misunderstandings. For example, Jenny communicated a partial message to Mike when she said, "Would you like to have lunch at Pepe's?" She left out her observations, opinions, feelings, and needs. Mike, thinking he was being asked a simple question, innocently said, "No." Had Jenny started out by expressing her observations, her opinions, her feelings, and her needs, it is likely that she and Mike would probably have had a pleasant Mexican lunch instead of an argument. Do you think Mike would have said no to the following whole message? "Mike, its three o'clock and we haven't eaten a thing since eight o'clock this morning (*observation*). I think it's unhealthy to go so long between meals (*opinion*). I don't know about you, but I'm starving. I'm getting cranky, tired, and weak too (*feelings*). I'd like to go to Pepe's to eat, relax, and just talk for an hour (*need*)."

Of course, not every relationship or situation requires whole messages. You can effectively express the symptoms of your ailing appliance to the repairman and spare him your feelings. Even with people you are close to, much of what you have to say is simply informational. You can decide when and with whom it is important to express yourself using whole messages.

EXERCISE: IDENTIFYING THE FOUR ELEMENTS OF A WHOLE MESSAGE

For each of the following partial messages, identify in the parentheses the three elements that are present, identify the missing element, and write a sentence to complete the whole message.

1. "This refrigerator sucks (_____)! It's alternating between freezing everything in the vegetable compartment and defrosting and leaking all over our kitchen floor. (_____). _____ (_____). Would you please clean up the puddle of water on the floor and call the repairman while I finish making dinner (_____)?"

2. "I got an email from your mother this morning inviting us to Florida for Christmas for the third year in a row (_____). We seem to be creating a family tradition of Christmas in Florida. (_____). While I like your folks, I regret not getting to be with my family at Christmas. (_____)

3. After work, Jan comes out to her car only to discover her car's battery is dead. She says to her coworker, "My car battery is dead (_____). I'm really upset (_____)! _____ (_____). Would you please give my car a jump if you have a set of cables (_____)?"

4. " _____ _____ (_____). I'm hurt and annoyed that you are making plans to redecorate our living room without consulting me (_____). If we redecorate the way you are suggesting, it would be too blah for me. (_____). Let's do this together, so we both have input about how our home looks (_____)."

Answers:

1. opinion; observation; "I'm really frustrated and angry. (*feeling*)"; need

2. observation; opinion; feeling; "I would prefer to stay home and be close to my family this Christmas. (*need*)"

3. observation; feeling; "I guess this old battery just isn't up to this cold weather we're having. (*opinion*)"; need

4. "So you plan to paint the whole house beige and get pastel furniture and white curtains. (*observation*)"; feeling; opinion; need

As you can see from this exercise, observations are facts that you have experienced, heard about, or read. Whole messages usually begin with a statement of your observations. Opinions, on the other hand, are what you conclude from your observations. Value judgments, beliefs, and theories are all types of conclusions.

Your feelings are a large part of what makes you unique and special. When you let others know what saddens, pleases, angers, and frightens you, they develop greater empathy for and understanding of you, and they are more apt to modify their behavior to meet your needs. Keep in mind that feeling statements are not observations or opinions. "I feel that you are ignoring me" is an example of a thinly veiled judgment.

You are the expert on what you need. Since no two people have the exact same needs, and nobody can read your mind, it is important to express your needs clearly. Needs are not judgmental or pejorative or blaming. They are simply statements about what would help you or please you.

EXERCISE: WRITE YOUR OWN WHOLE STATEMENT

Think of something that is important to you that you would like to communicate to someone else. Write a statement about it that includes your observation, your opinion, your feelings, and what you need.

"_____

_____ (observation).

_____

_____ (opinion).

_____

_____ (feelings).

_____

_____ (need)."

CONTAMINATED MESSAGES

Contaminated messages are different from partial messages in that part of the message is expressed covertly rather than just left out. Contaminated messages are particularly destructive when they are loaded with unexpressed negative emotions and needs. For instance, remember when Jenny shared her opinion with Mike: "Well, aren't you the busy little beaver? You never have time for us anymore. All you think about is work, work, work!" Her opinion is strongly tainted by unexpressed facts, feelings, and needs. Contaminated messages often result in alienation. Mike's response is understandable.

Contaminated messages are difficult to decipher because an important part of the message is covert. Here are three other examples of contaminated messages:

1. "You move like a snail!" This message is an opinion contaminated by covert observations, feelings, and needs. A whole message might have been, "I notice that you haven't brushed your hair or your teeth, and you are still eating your breakfast (*observations*). I think you better get up earlier from now on, so you won't be so rushed (*opinion*). I'm getting very impatient and irritated

(*feelings*). I want you to start walking to the bus stop right now so that I won't have to drive you to school and end up being late for work (*need*)."

2. "Did you get a hair cut, or did you get your ears lowered?" This message contaminates an observation with a opinion. The whole message might be "I noticed that you got your hair cut shorter than usual (*observation*). Everybody has different tastes. But from where I'm sitting, it looks a little light around the ears (*opinion*). I'm a little nervous about telling you this (*feelings*). I don't want you to be pissed off at me (*need*)."

3. "I can't believe you forgot our anniversary again!" This message is an opinion contaminated with covert feelings and needs. A whole message might be, "This is the second time in a row that you have forgotten our anniversary (*observation*). I don't think that you are making our marriage or me a high enough priority in your life (*opinion*). I feel unimportant to you. I'm really hurt and angry (*feelings*). I would like you to acknowledge how important I am to you by celebrating our wedding anniversary with me (*need*)."

Obviously there are times when you want to contaminate your messages for the fun of it. But when you are communicating something important to someone who matters to you, you can avoid misunderstandings and estrangement by making the content of your communication simple and straightforward. If you don't want to overtly state your feelings, be sure the tone of your voice conveys your emotions. For instance, the message "we need to get going" has a very different meaning depending on whether it is delivered in a matter-of-fact tone or an annoyed tone of voice. The key to avoiding contaminated messages is to separate out and express each part of the communication.

EXERCISE: CLEANING UP CONTAMINATED MESSAGES

Rewrite each of these contaminated messages as whole messages.

1. You are a customer at a restaurant and complain to waiter: "This fish is awful."

_____

_____

_____

2. You are talking to a fellow classmate who isn't doing his part on a class project that is due in three days: "You don't seem very enthusiastic about this project, Zack. What would it take to get you moving, a carrot or a stick of dynamite?"

_____

_____

_____

_____

3. You say to a classmate who just won a prestigious scholarship: "Of course you won it. All you ever did was study while we were playing ball and partying. How boring!"

_____

_____

_____

_____

4. You say to your neighbor: "Your goofball friends park in front of my place and broadcast their music to the entire neighborhood and blast their horn for at least ten minutes before you come out."

_____

_____

_____

_____

5. You are a supervisor talking to a worker: "I understand that your father died last month, but we're not paying you to sit on your thumbs. Either do your job or you're out of here."

_____

_____

_____

_____

Here are some examples of how to clean up the above contaminated messages.

1. "Waiter, this fish smells extremely fishy (*observation*). I'm getting nauseous and upset just having it in front of me (*feeling*). If I were to eat this, I know I would get seriously ill (*opinion*). I want you to take this back to the chef and bring me a hamburger (*need*)."

2. "Zack, this group project is due in three days. You've not done your part and we are finished with ours (*fact*). You're not making this a priority (*opinion*). We're really frustrated, angry, and worried about your inaction (*feeling*). We want you to get your part done on time (*need*)."

3. "I hear that you won a prestigious scholarship. You were studying in the library when we were playing ball and partying (*observation*). I find studying boring (*opinion*). I'm jealous and pissed off that you won (*feelings*). I wish I had won it (*need*)."

4. "When your friends come to pick you up, they park in front of my house and play loud music and honk their horn repeatedly. I can hear them way out back behind my house (*observation*). I think that's pretty darned inconsiderate (*opinion*). My blood starts to boil when my peace and quiet is disturbed (*feeling*). Would you please tell them to turn down their music and ring your doorbell when they come to get you (*need*)?"

5. "I understand that your father died last month (*observation*). I'm sorry to hear about that (*feeling*). I feel awkward about telling you that you need to get your job done or you're going to be fired (*feeling, need*). But I don't think it's fair that you come into work, accomplish next to nothing, and still expect to be paid (*opinion*)."

PREPARING WHOLE MESSAGES

Before you can express a whole message, you need to tune into yourself, the other person, and your environment.

What's Going On with You?

To better ensure that you are using whole messages instead of partial or contaminated messages, tune into your inner experience *before* you speak. Ask yourself:

1. What am I observing?

2. What am I thinking?

3. What am I feeling?

4. What do I want?

When you are first learning to express whole messages, you will find it useful to write down the answers to these questions, so that your message is clear and all parts of your message are distinct. Make a point of separating your observations from your beliefs and conclusions. Take responsibility for your opinion and come up with a way to phrase it that is not on the attack. Get in touch with your feelings and find a way to express them using "I messages." Think of a simple, nonthreatening way to say what you want.

What's Going On with the Other Person?

When you have something important to say to another person, it is always wise to consider what condition your listener is in. The moment your spouse walks in the door, exhausted and famished from a long day at work, would not be the best time to broach the subject of the fender bender you had·in the new family car. Try to pick a time to express important messages when your listener isn't distracted, irritable, hungry, tired, or upset.

Pay attention to how your listener is responding to you nonverbally as you share your message. Is she interested and open to what you have to say, or is she bored? Does he agree with you? Are you making good eye contact or is she looking away, or rolling her eyes? What do his facial expressions say? What does her body language express? Is he asking questions or giving you feedback, or is he silent?

Where Is a Good Place to Talk?

Choose a place to deliver important messages in which you and the other person have some privacy and are likely not to be interrupted. You will have a more receptive audience if the place you pick to talk is pleasant and relatively free of distractions. If you think that others are going to overhear your conversation, you are more likely to use partial or contaminated messages as you disguise your comments for any eavesdropper.

EXERCISE: WRITING WHOLE MESSAGES

In this exercise, you will practice writing a whole message to a person who matters to you. You can use the four basic questions to test whether it is a whole message:

1. Are you expressing the facts as you know them, based on what you've observed, read, or heard?

2. Are you clearly stating your opinion without attacking?

3. Are you sharing your feelings without blaming?

4. Are you conveying your needs without threatening?

Cindy scribbled down her first draft of a whole message to her husband and then asked herself the preceding questions and promptly rewrote it. Here is Cindy's first draft: "The weatherman said that we are in for heavy rain and wind tomorrow afternoon. I know I promised months ago to go to this game with you, but I think it is a dumb idea to go to the football game and sit there wet and cold. I'm staying home where it's warm and dry. If you must go and leave me home alone, maybe you can find someone to go with you who is as crazy as you are."

When Cindy reviewed this first draft, she noticed that she had stated the facts as she had heard them. But she allowed her negative feelings about getting wet and cold to contaminate her opinion about going to the game, and she implied that her husband was an idiot for going to the game in a storm. She also realized that she was blaming her husband for leaving her alone when she was the one who had decided to stay home. Here's how she revised the message: "The weatherman said that we are in for heavy rain and wind tomorrow afternoon. I hate getting wet and cold. I know I promised months ago to go to this game with you, but I think that it would be a bad idea for me to go in this storm. I would prefer to stay home with you, but I know how much you want to go. I bet you could ask one of your friends or your brother to go with you."

Now think of something important that you need to communicate to someone, and write a first draft of a whole message about it to this person:

_____

_____

_____

_____

Review what you've written, asking yourself the previously mentioned questions to test whether it is a whole message. If necessary, revise below:

_____

_____

_____

_____

EXERCISE: EXPRESSING WHOLE MESSAGES

Rehearse in your mind the whole message that you wrote in the preceding exercise. Practice saying it out loud in front of a mirror or tape record it to make sure that your nonverbal communication is consistent with your message. Choose a time and place to share your message that will maximize the likelihood that your message will be heard clearly. Pay attention to what is going on with the other person to determine the best time to talk and whether he or she is hearing your message as you intended.

Cindy practiced saying her revised whole message to her husband in her head and then said it out loud in front of the mirror. She noticed that taking ownership of her feelings, opinions, and needs allowed her to deliver a congruent message, free of sarcasm in her voice and blame in her words. She was able to deliver her message to her husband after dinner in a calm and firm voice, with good eye contact, and with a serious but friendly facial expression. He knew she meant what she said and therefore didn't try to talk her out of her decision. Instead, he headed for the phone to call his brother.

TWELVE COMMON PITFALLS

Here are twelve ways to express yourself that are most likely going to lead to trouble in your communicating with others.

Expecting People to Read Your Mind

You may fall into the trap of believing that what you think is fact and that others share your reality. You may therefore assume that you don't have to talk about the obvious. This is a myth. No two people think exactly alike, not even identical twins raised together. It is best to assume that the people in your life are poor mind readers and don't have a clue about what you are observing, thinking, feeling, and wanting.

Postponing What You Have to Say

When you are hurt, or angry or you want to change something, you may put off talking about it. You may walk away from the situation carrying on a dialogue in your head about what the other person said and what you should have said. This can only serve to fuel your frustration, hurt, and anger, but does nothing to help you get what you want. If you chronically postpone expressing your feelings, you are at risk of exploding over something major or minor.

When you speak up immediately, you can draw a connection between what others say and do and how it impacts you. You are able to teach people what you need so that they can adjust their behavior accordingly. You can enhance the intimacy between yourself and people who matter to you. Roger was attracted to his coworker Sandra and was hurt and annoyed when she didn't respond to him one day. He said, "Sandra, I just asked you a question and you acted as though I wasn't here. Things are pretty crazy around here right now, but I want you to know that that hurt my feelings. I don't care how busy you are. I still want you to acknowledge me. Is that too much to ask?" Immediate communication can clear up potential misunderstandings and enliven your relationships.

There are a couple of exceptions to the rule of immediate communication:

1. It is best to postpone communicating when you are very angry and likely to say or do something that you will regret later. While it is sometimes a good idea to cool off a bit and think about what you want to say before you share your feelings, don't wait indefinitely.

2. When you are being asked to respond to an important question and you are unsure of your answer, give yourself time to consider your thoughts, feelings, opinions, and needs.

Statements Masquerading As Questions

Asking a question rather than making a statement is a way of avoiding resistance and rejection. It works sometimes, for instance, when the other person happens to want the same thing that you do. But since this is often not the case, asking a question rather than making a direct statement can lead to unpleasant misunderstandings and you not getting what you want. Remember the example at the beginning of this chapter in which Jenny asked a seemingly innocent question, "Do you want to eat at Pepe's?" Hidden behind her question were the facts, her opinion, her feelings, and her needs. When she didn't make a clear statement that included these, her husband said no and honestly stated what he wanted. Jenny ended up in an argument and didn't get her needs met.

Expressing Incongruence

When the content of your message is not matched by the tone of your voice or your body language, people don't know what to believe. Sometimes people will take advantage of your incongruence to further their own agenda. For example, Laura said she didn't want to sign the petition thrust in front of her at the grocery store exit, but she continued to engage the petitioner in light conversation, to smile, and to not leave. It is no surprise that he thought she was interested and persisted in trying to convince her to sign.

People who know you well are more likely to take your incongruence as insincerity, and they are apt to feel put off by your mixed messages. For instance, at a family dinner, Linda announced her engagement to Sam. Her sister Alexandra was frowning and used a sarcastic tone of voice as she congratulated Linda. Linda knew immediately that Alexandra was not being honest, and she was at once puzzled, hurt, and angry.

Sending Double Messages

When you say two contradictory things at once, the effect is confusing, hurtful, and possibly annoying. One statement undercuts the other: "You did a beautiful job organizing this party. Too bad you didn't have people confirm if they were coming. There's a lot of untouched food and drinks. It must have put you back a bundle." "Come close, go away" and "I love you, I hate you" messages take a heavy toll on intimate relationships. For instance, a mother says to her toddler, "I love having you sit on my lap." And then adds, "You're such a wiggle worm, you're going to make bruises on my legs. Why can't you just sit still for once?"

Showing Sarcasm

Sarcasm is a form of humor that conveys an underlying message of contempt. It typically covers up feelings of anger or hurt and tends to create distance between you and your listener. For example, Alice had just spent the afternoon and much effort rearranging the living room when her husband got home. His reaction was, "Just great. I can use my new binoculars to watch the game on TV from the couch at the far end of the room. It'll feel like I'm right at the stadium."

Jumping from Topic to Topic

In the normal flow of conversation, it is usual to shift quickly from topic to topic. But when you need to talk about something important, it is best to focus on one thing at a time until you and your listener have stated clear whole messages that you both understand. For example, rather than sticking to the discussion about their plans for a Hawaiian vacation with his girlfriend, Mike shifted to talking about how cool it would be to scuba dive in the Great Barrier Reef and then went on to say how he wanted to go fishing in Alaska some day. His girlfriend became so frustrated that she responded by offering to plan their Hawaiian vacation by herself.

Dragging Up the Past

Not content to stay with the current problem, you build a case to prove you are right, based on every misdemeanor you can recall that is even vaguely related to the issue at hand. For example, rather than sticking to her annoyance about her husband spending too much time talking to a mutual woman friend at a party, Page recounted every example from their five-year marriage when he socialized "too much" with women friends.

Accusing with "You Messages"

This is when you attack your listener with opinions masquerading as fact and contaminated with feelings and needs: "You never help me with the baby." "You're impossible to reach by phone." "You say you care, but you really don't." In response to these accusations, the listener becomes defensive and possibly attacks back. "I messages," in which you take responsibility for your opinions, feelings, and needs, make it more likely your listener will be open to what you have to say. For example, "I have been cooped up with the baby all day. I'm so tense that I'm ready to scream. I really need you to watch the baby for an hour, so I can go out for a run. Okay?"

Using Global Negative Labels

You can instantly alienate people when you call them pejorative names, such as "you idiot!" or "You're a lazy, thoughtless bum!" Instead, use "I messages" and focus on specific behavior. For example, "I'm really upset with you for forgetting to file our income tax returns on time after we stayed up until two in the morning to finish them!"

Making Threats

A good way to end meaningful communication is to threaten to quit the job, end the relationship, withhold something valuable, or commit violence. Rather than discussing difficult issues until a mutually satisfying resolution is found, threatening a hostile action shifts the topic to what you will do if you don't get your way: "If you don't play my way, I'm going to take my marbles and go home!" When you feel the urge to deliver a threat, take a time-out instead. Give yourself some time to think of a whole message that is not attacking or threatening. If possible, come up with a win-win proposal: "I notice each game we play, you change the rules. I think that this is unfair, and I'm really frustrated and mad. I suggest that we alternate who gets to name the rules with each new game."

Playing the Adversarial Game

When the intent is to prove you're right or to win the debate, you are engaging in an adversarial game that is likely to end in an argument and emotional distance. You may get your way or win your point in the short run. But your "winning" puts the other person in the position of losing, and this often creates enmity. When you find yourself feeling defensive and wanting to criticize the other person, you are playing the adversarial game: "No, I did not leave the water running. I wasn't even in the backyard today. You were here all day. You know that you are absentminded and are always blaming me for mistakes that you have made."

Supportive communication, in which there is mutual respect and sharing, leads to understanding and closeness. You can avoid or break out of an adversarial game by using whole messages.

For example, instead of becoming adversarial when your partner asks if you left the water running in the backyard, you might say: "I don't think I did (*opinion*), since I don't recall being in the backyard today (*observation*). I'm feeling irritated and defensive (*feelings*) when you ask me if I left the water on. Rather than trying to convince you I didn't leave the water on, I want to understand why you think I did leave it on (*need*)." After patiently listening to your partner's reasoning, you might gently say: "I want to ask you if there is another possible explanation as to why the water was on?" At this point your partner is likely to admit she or he is possibly the one who left the water on. At the end of this discussion, nobody has won or lost. Only water, not hard feelings, has been spilled.

EXERCISE: IDENTIFY AND AVOID THE TWELVE COMMON PITFALLS OF EXPRESSING

Review each pitfall, and on a separate piece of paper write down an example of it from your life. Then rewrite how you could have expressed yourself more effectively, using the skills that you have learned in this chapter.

WHOLE MESSAGES TAKE PRACTICE

In this chapter you have learned to express whole messages to people who are significant in your life. While you are still learning this skill, you should write down your whole message (observations, along with your opinion, feelings, and needs) before you share it with the person it is intended for. This will minimize partial and contaminated messages. You can rehearse your script in your mind or out loud in front of a mirror to make sure that your nonverbal communication matches your words. All of this requires that you pay attention to what's going on inside you. It is also important to be sensitive to what's going on with the other person. Be careful not to fall into the twelve common pitfalls of expressing yourself.

PART 2

Handling Difficult
Conversations and Situations

CHAPTER 4

Regulating Your Emotions: Managing Intense Anger

Jodie was an attractive, intelligent, hard-working woman with a successful career in banking. At thirty-four, she was one of the youngest international managers in her bank, and although she spent most of her time alone in her office, she loved her work. Jodie's social life was less fulfilling. She had few friends and was not in a relationship. She met people easily enough, men and women. But within a short time, she would inevitably find herself feeling let down, disappointed in their behavior, and generally unwilling to put up with what seemed to be glaring shortcomings. She would feel justified in her anger, and if she didn't break off the friendship or relationship first, the other person usually did after experiencing the full brunt of Jodie's displeasure.

It was as her most recent relationship (at two months a relatively long one for Jodie) was ending that Jodie began to think that this pattern might not have to continue forever. Her departing boyfriend, after surviving a furious tirade from Jodie, remarked—equally furiously—that she would benefit from some help with her emotions, and the sooner the better.

HANDLING NEGATIVE EMOTIONS

Learning how to handle your negative emotions when you are stressed can help you

- communicate more effectively

- get your needs met

- improve your interactions with others at home and at work

- decrease conflict and increase intimacy in your relationships

You may know all the skills in this book and be able to practice them successfully in a nonstressful environment, but the minute your emotional arousal level begins to increase, you may find yourself unable to even listen, much less able to express yourself and negotiate. Of all negative emotions, anger is by far the most difficult to regulate. This is partly because an angry outburst can feel—in the short term—extremely rewarding. In the short term, you release an intense buildup of emotion and may intimidate others into giving you what you want. Anger is also a "garbage can" kind of feeling: it's usually triggered by other painful feelings, often as a defense against the powerlessness of those underlying feelings. Only by managing your anger can you free yourself to use the communication skills that you've acquired.

WHAT IS EMOTION?

When people have an intense negative feeling or emotion, they experience a surge of adrenaline, an increase of physical tension, or a rush of thoughts. But they may have difficulty describing what the underlying feeling actually is. Is it fear? frustration? disappointment? embarrassment? Without this important information, you cannot communicate fully about yourself and your experience, and your relationships will inevitably suffer.

EXERCISE: DESCRIBING YOUR EMOTIONS

Start practicing using words for what you feel so that you can then communicate this important information about yourself. On the simplest level, you can describe yourself as feeling mad, glad, sad, or bad. Each of these categories can be further differentiated into many other feelings. Since this chapter is about painful emotions, this exercise addresses the mad, sad, and bad feelings. Think about some recent events where you experienced some uncomfortable feelings. Then, using the list of words below, identify and circle the feeling (or feelings) that best reflects that experience.

Mad	Sad	Bad
angry	defeated	afraid
annoyed	dejected	anxious
enraged	depressed	bored
frustrated	despairing	confused
furious	disappointed	desperate
impatient	discouraged	embarrassed
irked	gloomy	guilty
irritated	hopeless	helpless
livid	lonely	horrified

resentful	miserable	humiliated
violated	pessimistic	isolated
	resigned	needy
	unappreciated	overwhelmed
	unfulfilled	panicky
	unloved	pressured
	vulnerable	stuck
		threatened
		trapped
		uneasy
		upset
		worried

Now read the following half-sentences, and insert the feeling word or words that you imagine would best describe your reaction in each hypothetical situation.

1. "When you told me that you'd call me last night, and you didn't, I felt _____
_____."

2. "When the boss criticized me in front of the whole team, I felt _____
_____."

3. "When I realized that I'd sent in the wrong application form for the position, I felt _____
_____."

4. "When I saw the group of men standing on the sidewalk in front of me, I felt _____
_____."

5. "When you told me to 'shut up' at dinner tonight, I felt _____
_____."

6. "When I found your wedding ring lying on the dresser instead of on your finger, I felt _____
_____."

7. "When Dad announced that he was moving to Florida, I felt _____
_____."

8. "When you decided to use your bonus check to replace your golf clubs, I felt _____
_____."

If you responded to the majority of the statements with the word "anger," go back over the list and try to identify some other emotions you might experience under these circumstances. You might not feel them as strongly as you would feel anger, but write them down anyway.

Possible answers:

1. disappointed, sad, rejected

2. embarrassed, humiliated

3. frustrated, disappointed

4. terrified, helpless

5. resentful

6. betrayed, afraid

7. abandoned, lonely

8. disappointed, resentful, unimportant

WHAT IS THE FUNCTION OF EMOTION?

Emotions provide information to you about what's going on in any particular situation so that you can make appropriate decisions about how to respond. Strong emotions however, like anger, *impel you to take action* and short-circuit the decision-making process. When you're angry, your anger makes you want to attack, to lash out at whoever or whatever you see as being responsible for your pain. Although at the time this can feel like an enormous relief, it can be devastating to your relationships.

EXERCISE: IDENTIFYING ANGER-IMPELLED BEHAVIOR

Review some recent times you felt angry or upset. Describe the situation. Then, regardless of how you actually responded to the situation, write down what you wanted to say.

Here's how Daniel completed the exercise:

1. **Describe the situation:** "Terrence (my seventeen-year-old son) brought the car home an hour after curfew. I'd been waiting up for him, scared to death."

   What did you want to say? "You irresponsible, ungrateful little turd. You don't care about anyone but yourself, and I'm sick and tired of it. It's going to be a cold day in hell before I lend you the car again."

2. **Describe the situation:** "My boss said he'd give me the Maritime account, and then he went and gave it to Phillips."

   What did you want to say? "You rotten, lying jerk. You don't deserve my loyalty, and now you're not going to get it."

3. **Describe the situation:** "My wife forgot to pay the insurance bill on time so now there's a hefty surcharge."

   What did you want to say? "If you could just keep track of the bills as well as you keep track of your stupid luncheon dates, we'd be fine."

Now think of some times when you've been angry or upset, and fill in the blanks.

1. Describe the situation: _____

   _____

   What did you want to say? _____

   _____

2. Describe the situation: _____

   _____

   What did you want to say? _____

   _____

3. Describe the situation: _____

   _____

   What did you want to say? _____

   _____

If you're like most people, you wanted to say something blaming (someone else made you feel this way), you labeled the person or thing you saw as responsible for your pain as bad (an idiot, stupid, a jerk, selfish, etc.), you suggested that there was an intent to cause you pain (despite knowing how much you hate the behavior in question), or you magnified the situation until it felt completely intolerable.

"You %$#&@*! I can't believe you did that to me again! This is the end!" is an example of all four: blaming, labeling, implying intent, and magnifying.

ANGER AS A SECONDARY EMOTION

Lots of times when you're angry and on the attack, there's pain underneath the anger. Sometimes anger is triggered to hide the helpless feelings associated with pain and to replace them with the more powerful experience of anger. If you're threatened by a mugger, you may feel anger, but in all likelihood, underneath the anger you have more painful feelings of fear and helplessness. If your lover abruptly decides to end the relationship, you may again feel anger, but probably underneath the anger you have feelings of sadness, grief, even unworthiness. In these circumstances, anger is not the primary emotion that's triggered by the situation itself, but the secondary emotion that gets triggered by (or defends against) the underlying painful emotion.

Secondary emotions are the emotions triggered by your reactions to and interpretations of your primary emotions. If you speak to others who have experienced being mugged, and they report having felt only rage, you may interpret your fear and helplessness as a humiliating demonstration of wimpiness, and feel secondary emotions of humiliation and shame as well as anger. So anger as a secondary emotion is also prompted by thoughts and assumptions about how you *should* be feeling about something, and about how others are viewing you. All experiences of anger can be taken as a cue to investigate what the underlying primary emotions might be.

EXERCISE: IDENTIFYING ANGER AND THE UNDERLYING PRIMARY PAIN

Examine how Alison filled out the chart below, and then use the blank template to record times you've felt angry and on the attack and to identify the underlying pain.

What happened?	How did you feel?	Underlying pain?
Vassily said he was going to come by tonight, but he didn't, and he didn't call.	Terrible: angry and definitely on the attack. (He's so rude and irresponsible.)	Hurt and disappointed
Karen didn't have the copies of the documents ready on time for my meeting.	Furious (I gave her three days; I can't believe she didn't get them done.)	Worried about how my presentation would be received without them
Mom called to say that she and Dad were leaving tomorrow to see my sister in Seattle.	Frustrated and angry (why do they always tell me at the last minute?)	Hurt that they don't keep in touch more about their plans and jealous that they don't come and see me as often as they see my sister
Vassily didn't introduce me to his friends whom we met at the concert. He just yacked away while I stood looking like a fool.	Angry	Embarrassed and unimportant and left out
My boss hired someone from the outside to take the managerial position I'd applied for.	Enraged (All these years I've worked for him; he knew I wanted that position and deserved it, too.)	Resentful, unappreciated, and trapped

Now fill out your own chart, describing several situations, the angry feelings that were triggered, and the underlying painful feelings. Use new situations as they occur, or review your history for other relevant incidents.

What happened?	How did you feel?	Underlying pain?

OPPOSITE ACTION

When you indulge in the impulse to attack, you may feel a fleeting sense of power, of strength (which in the short term may reinforce your angry response), but it's at a huge cost. Over time, your relationships will suffer, and ultimately the damage will be irreparable. Friendships and love relationships will be lost; work relationships will cool. Most importantly, attacking with anger doesn't really decrease your emotional pain. Giving way to angry impulses actually tends to increase your anger and harden your angry attitude. And each angry outburst makes it more likely that you'll respond next time with anger, reinforcing the negative cycle. Physiologically, anger isn't healthy either. Anger and hostility have been associated with high blood pressure, heart disease, and digestive problems for years. There have even been suggestions of a relationship between anger and certain types of cancer.

Marsha Linehan (1993) describes the process of "opposite action" as an approach to reduce emotional pain. The idea is you can choose to do the opposite of what your impulse dictates. When you act directly opposite to your impulse, you rob your anger of the reinforcement such powerful outbursts provide, and your feelings will often change accordingly.

Once you can identify the primary painful feelings that underlie your anger, the choice to react differently becomes easier to make. Of course, if your feelings are an appropriate response to a potentially dangerous situation, then taking opposite action won't be a useful strategy. For example, if someone is physically threatening you, anger can provide the energy to mobilize against that person, so anger *is* therefore the appropriate response. Opposite action is most useful when you perceive your feelings to be an overreaction, when those feelings are keeping you from accomplishing things that are important to you, or when they are not helpful under the circumstances, even if appropriate.

Designing an opposite action in the face of anger and the impulse to attack is a skill that requires empathy and compassion. It involves trying to understand the other person's experience, fears, and needs, and acknowledging those feelings and needs. It includes finding a way to appreciate others for who they are, with all their human frailties and limitations.

EXERCISE: STAND IN THEIR SHOES: GAINING EMPATHY AND UNDERSTANDING

The exercise that follows, adapted from McKay, Rogers, and McKay (1989), will enable you to gain a sense of empathy for the person you're angry at. Standing in the other person's shoes is an essential step in defining an opposite action and enabling you to regulate your anger. First read how Michelene completed the exercise. Then you'll have a chance to answer your own questions.

Here is how Michelene described a recent situation:

What happened? "I'd made a point to ask Don to be sure to supervise the kids' homework while I was at Mom's after her surgery. It was just for a few days, but at this age when they fall behind it's really hard to catch up. When I got back, the kids showed me what they'd done, and it was barely anything. They both said Dad hadn't done it with them at all. And on top of that, the house was a mess, the kitchen filthy. Don and I had a great big fight about it."

What did you want to say to him or her? "I told him that I couldn't count on him for even the smallest responsibility and that it was like having another child in the house. I said that I'm sick and tired of having to take care of everything all the time."

What was the other person feeling? "Don was probably feeling overwhelmed by having to take care of the kids while I was away. He usually just has to go to work and come home and pretty much everything is taken care of. I guess he might have been somewhat worried about how I was doing, since I was pretty scared about Mom's surgery. And I imagine that he was probably feeling a little abandoned because he's used to me taking such good care of him, and he often says that makes him feel loved."

What were his or her needs that might have led to—or influenced—this behavior? "Don needs a certain amount of downtime every day to cope with the stresses of his job. It's true, his job is very stressful. I wouldn't want to have to deal with what he does every day. And because he works with people every day, some of that downtime needs to be alone time. I imagine that because he had to leave work early to get the kids he probably had to work at night after they were in bed just to keep up. He also really likes to be pampered a little—I guess that's actually a need too, not just a like."

What beliefs or values might be contributing to this behavior? "He definitely has some old-fashioned beliefs about the division of labor around the house. The kids are usually my domain, though he does help with getting them ready for school, taking them to their sports events, and stuff like that. I imagine that he also believes deep down that since he works longer hours and makes more money than I do his work is more important and he's more entitled to relaxation time. I don't really agree, but I see his point."

What do you know about this person's past experiences or history that might be influencing him or her to act in this way? "Don's mom took care of everything in his house. After his dad died when Don was ten, his mom went to work full-time, but she still made sure to have dinner cooked every night, helped him with homework, and so on. And she had five kids! I don't know how she did it. Even now she's a bundle of energy at seventy-six."

What limitations might be influencing him or her to act this way? "Don really doesn't deal very well with typical household chaos. I know he feels easily overwhelmed when the kids run around or when they're not going about things the way he thinks they should. Getting the kids up and ready in the morning is a stretch for him; getting dinner cooked at night is probably sorely testing his limits. He has a bad back too, and it's possible that his back started giving him trouble with all the added stress. So I guess that supervising homework just didn't even make it to his radar screen. I discovered that the kids didn't bathe while I was away either; that didn't make it to Don's radar screen either. It's just as well neither of them had soccer practice."

Okay, now it's your turn. Think about the last time you were angry at someone.

Describe briefly what happened: _____

_____

_____

What did you want to say to him or her? _____

_____

_____

Now think about the following questions and write your answers to the best of your ability in the spaces provided. If you don't know the exact answer, make up something that seems plausible. Remember, the goal of the exercise is to understand the interaction from the other person's point of view.

What was the other person feeling? _____

_____

What were the person's needs that might have led to—or influenced—his or her behavior? _____

_____

_____

What beliefs or values might be contributing to this behavior? _____

_____

_____

_____

What do you know about this person's past experiences or history that might be influencing him or her to act this way (including rewards, successes, failures, hurts, and losses)? _____

_____

_____

_____

_____

What limitations (fears, health problems, lack of skills) might be influencing him or her to act this way?

_____

_____

_____

_____

Once you've begun empathizing with the other person, it's necessary to develop a verbal acknowledgment of their experience that's compassionate and appreciative. This is the core of opposite action, a response that is incompatible with anger.

EXERCISE: DEVELOPING AN OPPOSITE ACTION STATEMENT

As a follow-up to the previous exercise, write a statement that summarizes the other person's feelings and needs in a way that shows compassion and understanding for their behavior. Before you write your own, see how Michelene composed her opposite action statement.

Michelene's statement: "Don, I imagine that you were really stressed and overwhelmed by all the responsibilities that you had to take on while I was away, on top of your own taxing job. And I suppose that you were probably worried about me and mom as well. I know you need your downtime too, and having the kids full-time just doesn't allow for that. I appreciate your allowing me to go spend the time with mom and can understand why supervising the kids' homework wouldn't have been at the top of your priority list."

Your own opposite action statement: _____

_____

_____

_____

_____

The success of opposite action is in its repetition. Think about other times in the recent past when you've been angry at someone. For each incident, go through the last two exercises to gain empathy and develop an opposite action statement.

SUMMING IT UP

Once you've practiced the skills in this chapter, you can practice them at home or at work or in any situation where they would apply. The scenario would begin with some incident or situation where you feel angry. Instead of automatically responding with a verbal attack, step one is to recognize that you're angry and to notice what you want to do (the impulse to attack). Step two is to differentiate between the anger and the secondary underlying pain. Step three is to focus on empathizing with the person whose behavior you don't like so that you can undermine your automatic angry response. Then, step four is to develop an opposite action statement.

EXERCISE: ONE, TWO, THREE, FOUR

Fred had worked for the same company for twelve years, and he was a hard-working and loyal employee. His boss, Jerry, had recently told him that if he completed the annual accounting report on time, he would get a raise. Fred had worked like crazy for six weeks, working at night and on weekends to get the report finished, and he had been successful. But after two months, he'd seen no sign of a raise. When he approached Jerry about it, his boss brushed him off with irritated reassurances that weren't reassuring to Fred. He completed the exercise in the following way:

1. **What are your feelings and what do you want to do or say?** "I'm enraged at him and I feel like quitting, but only after I tell him what a sad-ass loser of a boss he is and how I wouldn't stay with him if my life depended on it. I can think of some other juicy things to say too and wouldn't mind trashing my files, just for emphasis."

2. **What is the secondary underlying pain?** "Okay, underneath the anger, I guess, is disappointment that my hard work hasn't been rewarded as promised. But more than that, I feel betrayed. I've put such a lot of hard work into this job and thought it was appreciated. The way Jerry's treating me says to me that I'm just not important."

3. **How do you understand the other person's behavior?** "Jerry's been having some personal problems lately. His son was recently arrested for possession of drugs and he's starting a rehab program soon. I imagine Jerry and his wife are both pretty preoccupied with that situation. I imagine all he wants is for the business to run smoothly for a while until he can focus on it again. I suppose I can be patient a little longer."

4. **Fred's opposite action statement:** "Jerry, I know you're dealing with a lot lately, and I imagine that your attention is more on how to help your son than on anything here. I've felt well-supported by you in the past, so I understand that although my raise isn't high on your priority list, it doesn't mean that you aren't appreciative of my work."

Now complete the same exercise. Use an incident that you're currently angry about, or one from the past.

1. What are your feelings and what do you want to do or say? _____

_____

_____

_____

2. What is the secondary underlying pain? _____

_____

_____

_____

3. How do you understand the other person's behavior? _____

_____

_____

_____

4. Your opposite action statement: _____

_____

_____

_____

The key to success in emotional regulation is practice, practice, and more practice. In time, the skills described in this chapter will come more easily and will eventually begin to replace your automatic angry responses.

CHAPTER 5

Asserting Yourself: The Middle Way between Aggressive and Passive Styles

The benefits of assertive communication include

- expressing your opinion and feelings without alienating others

- stating and defending what you want and don't want

- dealing effectively with criticism and resistance

- maintaining mutual respect and self-esteem

In assertive communication, the underlying assumption is that while you and I may have our differences, we are equally entitled to express ourselves respectfully to one another and defend our respective rights.

With *passive communication*, you express yourself indirectly or withhold your point of view, feelings, and needs. You often don't get what you want and are frustrated. When you engage in *aggressive communication*, you speak your mind, and nobody is in doubt about how you feel or what you want, but you ignore other people's feelings, opinions, and rights. You often get what you want in the short run, but you also succeed in alienating everyone around you.

WHAT ARE YOUR LEGITIMATE RIGHTS?

As a child, you learned from your parents and other role models a set of assumptions about what was good and what was bad. While many of your beliefs from childhood may still be useful to you, some of your traditional assumptions may actually violate your legitimate rights as an adult. You can decide for yourself which of your traditional assumptions are still useful and which interfere with your being an assertive adult. The following exercise, adapted from Davis, Eshelman, and McKay (2000), will help.

EXERCISE: QUESTIONING TRADITIONAL ASSUMPTIONS

Read the following list of traditional assumptions. Put a check mark in the "then" column by the assumptions that remind you of the rules you learned as a child. Then put a check mark in the "now" column by the assumptions that you still believe apply to you. Listed beside each traditional assumption is a statement of your legitimate right as an adult. These rights are a reminder that you are an adult with alternatives.

Your Traditional Assumptions			Your Legitimate Rights
Then	Now		
1. ____	____	It is selfish to put your needs before the needs of others.	You have a right to put yourself first sometimes.
2. ____	____	It is shameful to make mistakes.	You have a right to make mistakes.
3. ____	____	If you can't convince others that your feelings are reasonable, then your feelings must be wrong.	You have a right to be the final judge of your feelings and accept them as legitimate.
4. ____	____	You should respect the views of others, especially if they are in a position of authority. Keep your differences of opinion to yourself.	You have a right to have your own opinions and convictions.
5. ____	____	You should always try to be logical and consistent.	You have a right to change your mind or decide on a different course of action.
6. ____	____	You should be flexible and adjust. Others have good reasons for their actions and it's not polite to question them.	You have a right to protest any treatment or criticism that feels bad to you.
7. ____	____	You should never interrupt people. Asking questions reveals your stupidity to others.	You have a right to interrupt in order to ask for clarification.

8. ____	____	Things could get even worse; don't rock the boat.	You have a right to negotiate for change.
9. ____	____	You shouldn't take up others' valuable time with your problems.	You have a right to ask for help or emotional support.
10. ____	____	People don't want to hear that you feel bad, so keep it to yourself.	You have a right to feel and express pain.
11. ____	____	When someone takes the time to give you advice, you should take it very seriously.	You have a right to ignore the advice of others.
12. ____	____	Doing something well is its own reward. People don't like showoffs. Be modest when complimented.	You have a right to receive recognition for your work and achievements.
13. ____	____	You should always try to accommodate others. If you don't, they won't be there when you need them.	You have a right to say no.
14. ____	____	Don't be antisocial. People are going to think you don't like them if you say you'd rather be alone instead of with them.	You have a right to be alone, even if others would prefer you spend time with them.
15. ____	____	You should always have a good reason for what you feel and do.	You have a right to not have to justify yourself to others.
16. ____	____	When someone is in trouble, you should always help them.	You have a right to not take responsibility for someone else's problem.
17. ____	____	You should be sensitive to the needs and wishes of others, even when they are unable to tell you what they want.	You have a right not to have to anticipate the needs and wishes of others.
18. ____	____	It's not nice to put people off. If questioned, give an answer.	You have a right to choose to not respond to a situation.

IDENTIFYING THREE BASIC STYLES OF COMMUNICATION

Now that you know your legitimate rights, you can examine more closely the difference between passive, aggressive, and assertive communication. You will then be ready to identify which of the three styles of communication you are using at any given time.

Passive Style

When you are in a passive mode, you express your opinions, feelings, and wants indirectly, by frowning, crying, sighing, yawning, or whispering something under your breath. You tend to rely on others to guess what you want to say. Your needs come second. When you do speak up, you throw in disclaimers such as "I'm no expert" and "I probably shouldn't be saying this." It's difficult for you to ask for what you want or to say no.

When you are being passive, your voice may be soft, even wavering. You may be vague; you may ramble, speak with many pauses, and use phrases such as "I mean" and "you know." Your posture is likely to be slouched. When feeling forced to speak, you are nervous and fidgety. Making eye contact may be hard for you.

The underlying message in passive communication is "I'm weak and inferior, and you're powerful and right." The major advantage of passive communication is that it minimizes your responsibility for making decisions and eliminates the risk associated with taking a personal stand on an issue. There are also some major disadvantages to passive communication, mainly a sense of impotence, lowered self-esteem, and the fact that you have to live with the decisions of others.

EXERCISE: IDENTIFYING YOUR OWN PASSIVE COMMUNICATION

Read the following example of passive communication and then write down an example from your own life.

Jane's example:

I behaved passively in this situation: *In a restaurant during dinner*

With this person: *The waiter*

What I said: *"The vegetables and rice are great"*

What I did: *I kept quiet about the fact I had ordered my steak well done, and it came rare, so I could only eat the cooked outside part.*

The advantages of being passive in this situation: *Not making a scene and embarrassing myself in front of my friends.*

The disadvantages: *I paid for my meal and went home hungry and mad at myself for not speaking up.*

Your example:

I behaved passively in this situation: _____

With this person: _____

What I said: _____

What I did: _____

The advantages of being passive in this situation were: _____

_____

The disadvantages: _____

_____

Aggressive Style

When you are in an aggressive mode, it is easy to express your opinion, feelings, and wants, but you often do so at the expense of others' rights and feelings. Your sarcasm and humorous put-downs humiliate others. When you are not getting your way, you go on the attack and blame others for not meeting your needs. You are an expert in the use of "you messages" followed by a criticism or negative label. You also use absolute terms such as "always" and "never" to underscore that you are absolutely right.

When you are being aggressive, you have command of a broad range of vocal alternatives, from "dead silence" to flip and sarcastic remarks, to screaming rage. Your eyes may be narrow and expressionless. When really angry, your face reddens, and your muscles become taut. Your posture is that of a rock: feet firmly planted, hands on hips, jaw clenched and jutting out, gestures rigid, abrupt, and intimidating. You may point your finger, make a fist, or pound the table to punctuate what you have to say.

The underlying message in an aggressive communication is "I'm superior and right, and you're inferior and wrong." The advantage of aggressive behavior is that people often give you what you want to get rid of you. The major disadvantages are that it engenders resentment, causes others to be devious to avoid a confrontation, and creates uncooperative enemies in the future.

EXERCISE: IDENTIFYING YOUR OWN AGGRESSIVE COMMUNICATION

Read the following example of aggressive communication and then write down an example from your own life.

Jim's example:

I behaved aggressively in this situation: *In the car with my wife driving*

With this person: *My wife (who was driving)*

What I said: *"Are you blind? Can't you see the brake lights of the car in front of us? You never brake in time. Pull over and let me drive. You almost killed us. You never pay attention, and then you have to brake too hard. You are the worst driver I've ever seen."*

What I did: *I yelled at her, and I got really red and tense.*

The advantages of being aggressive in this situation: *My wife drove more carefully, and I felt safer.*

The disadvantages: *My wife didn't speak to me for a day after that, and now she refuses to drive with me in the car.*

Your example:

I behaved aggressively in this situation: _____

With this person: _____

What I said: _____

What I did: _____

The advantages of being aggressive in this situation: _____

_____

The disadvantages: _____

_____

Assertive Style

When you are in an assertive mode, you are able to defend your own opinions, feelings, and needs, using direct "I statements," while taking into account the rights and feelings of others. You listen to other points of view, and let people know that you have heard them. You ask for what you want and set limits. You give and receive compliments. You respond firmly to criticism and disagreements.

EXERCISE: SETTING GOALS TO BE ASSERTIVE

Write down three social situations in your life in which you would like to be assertive. Remember your legitimate rights as an adult. Who are the people in each situation with whom you want to be assertive? How would you like your behavior to be different? Be very specific. Don't worry about your feelings at this point. Your feelings will naturally change as you behave differently and get positive results in real life.

First look at the example, and then write down your own goals.

John's assertiveness goals:

1. I want to tell my boss no when he asks me to stay late on Friday nights.

2. I want to share my opinions about company policy with my colleagues at staff meetings.

3. I would like to ask a new friend, Susan, to go with me to the movies.

Your assertiveness goals:

1. _____

2. _____

3. _____

HOW TO MAKE AN ASSERTIVE POSITION STATEMENT

When you want to take a stand on a specific issue, use an *assertive position statement*. The issue may be a small one, such as where to have dinner with your mate, in which case you can spontaneously express yourself. When you have a big issue, such as whether to buy a new car, it is best to set aside a mutually agreed upon time to talk: "Joanie, I've been thinking about buying a new car; is this a good time to talk?. . . No. . . . Well how about tonight after dinner?. . . Okay." In any event, you need to express your position clearly and fully because partial communication can lead to misunderstandings and frustration.

An assertive position statement includes three essential pieces of information:

1. Your perspective of the situation

2. Your feelings about the situation

3. What you want

These three pieces of information reveal exactly where you stand on an issue. Stating your definition of the problem or how you see the situation is necessary for focusing the discussion. Here is your opportunity to share the facts as you see them and your opinion regarding the issue at hand. For example: "It's time to make a decision about where we're going to eat tonight. I know you love Mexican food, but we've eaten at Tijuana Joe's the last three times we've gone out for dinner. We're in a rut!"

Sharing your feelings gives the other person a better understanding of how important an issue is to you. Do not substitute an opinion for a feeling ("I feel that Mexican food should be abolished!") An example of a feeling statement is, "I'm really tired of Mexican food." Once they are expressed, your feelings can often play a major role in helping you get what you want, especially when your opinion differs markedly from that of your listener. If nothing else, your listener may be able to relate to and understand your feelings about an issue, even when he or she totally disagrees with your perspective. When you share all your feelings, you become less of an adversary.

Define what you want in a simple sentence that is very specific, such as, "I would like to go to that new fish place tonight."

Here are two examples of assertive position statements:

1. "Julie, Thank you for inviting me to join the Christmas boutique committee. I know you need all the help you can get. I have participated in it every year since I joined the church. While part of me feels disloyal for not being involved this year, I mostly feel relief in not over-committing myself for once and ending up hating the entire season. So this year, I'm saying no."

2. "I've noticed that you've been late to our staff meeting several weeks running. We end up having to stop the meeting to fill you in. I'm really getting annoyed with this pattern. I would appreciate your making a point of getting here on time from now on."

Notice that these assertive statements do not blame or use attacking labels. The situation is described specifically and objectively. By using "I messages" rather than "you messages," the speaker owns his opinions, feelings, and wants. The listener is unlikely to become defensive, tune out to what you are saying, or prepare a counterattack or retreat.

When you are expressing yourself assertively, you convey an air of strength and empathy. Your voice is relaxed, well-modulated, and firm. While you are comfortable with direct eye contact, you don't stare. Your eyes communicate openness and honesty. Your posture is balanced and erect.

EXERCISE: WRITING ASSERTIVE POSITION STATEMENTS

Review the last exercise, in which you set goals to be assertive in three situations. Use the following three-step format to write an assertive position statement for each situation. Take time to clarify for yourself each component of your assertive position statements. Write each statement on a separate piece of paper if you want to elaborate on your responses. You may need to review your legitimate rights if you find it difficult to imagine yourself expressing what you really think, feel, and want.

Fill in the blanks below.

1. "I think _____."

   "I feel _____."

   "I want _____."

2. "I think _____."

   "I feel _____."

   "I want _____."

3. "I think _____."

   "I feel _____."

   "I want _____."

EXERCISE: REHEARSE YOUR ASSERTIVE POSITION STATEMENTS

Practice reading your statements in front of a mirror. Pay attention to the volume and tone of your voice, as well as your posture, gestures, and facial expressions. Develop a congruent message. Rehearse your statements until you can say them without any written prompts.

EXERCISE: USING YOUR IMAGINATION

Imagine actually delivering an assertive position statement to the person for whom it is intended. Imagine the person's response. Prepare an assertive comeback to what you anticipate the response to be. First look at the example dialogue and then write down your own assertive dialogue on a separate piece of paper.

Cindy imagined the following scenario with her roommate:

Cindy: I notice that the food I stored for this week in the refrigerator, before I left for the weekend, is gone. I'm really annoyed, and I would like you to replace it before I get home tonight.

Ed: Miss Perfect, like you never eat any of my food! Just last week you finished off my Chinese takeout.

Cindy: That was wrong and I won't do it again. I'm asking you again to replace my week's supply of food before I get home tonight so that I won't have to shop today.

Ed: I don't have time to shop until tomorrow. I'll just give you the money, and you go get what I took.

Cindy: No, I'm willing to wait until tomorrow for you to replace my food. I'll eat out tonight.

Ed: Okay, okay. Boy, you sure aren't the nice little Cindy you used to be.

Cindy: No, I'm not.

EXERCISE: ROLE-PLAYING

Practice role-playing, making your assertive position statement, with a supportive friend. You can ask your friend to pretend to be the person for whom the statement is intended. Your friend can respond as you would expect that person to respond. This will help you to develop good responses to any resistance you anticipate.

EXERCISE: EXPRESSING YOURSELF IN REAL LIFE

Deliver your assertive position statement to the person for whom it was intended. You can use other assertiveness skills described later in this chapter to deal with the person's response should he or she become critical or throw you off track. Even if the person remains uncooperative, you get the opportunity to practice being assertive and to take pride in defending your rights.

DEALING WITH CRITICISM

Many people have difficulty dealing with criticism. If this is true for you, review your legitimate rights at the beginning of this chapter before you go on with this section. In short, while others are entitled to their opinions, feelings, and wishes; you have a right to ask them to respect yours. Three assertive strategies for responding to criticism are acknowledgment, clouding, and probing.

Acknowledgment

When someone offers constructive criticism, you can use this feedback to improve yourself. When you have made a mistake, having someone point it out to you can be helpful in preventing future errors. When you receive criticism with which you agree, whether it is constructive or simply a reminder, acknowledge that the critic is right. An example would be, "Yes, I did manage to put on one navy and one black sock this morning. Thanks for pointing it out."

You don't have to give an excuse or apologize for your behavior. Everyone makes mistakes. As an adult, you can choose to explain your behavior, but you do not need to. Ask yourself if you want to or if you are just explaining yourself out of habit.

If you think that your critic is sincerely trying to give you constructive criticism, and the two of you simply disagree, you can assertively acknowledge your critic's perspective and then share yours. For example, "I hear that in your opinion I'm doing this incorrectly. I see things differently. You're entitled to your opinion. Please respect mine."

EXERCISE: RESPONDING TO CONSTRUCTIVE CRITICISM

Read the following examples of how Sara, Don, and Judy each acknowledged criticism, and then compose an acknowledgment of your own in response to some constructive criticism you have experienced in your life.

Critic: Your hair is messy.

Sara: You're right, it is messy.

Critic: You don't make good eye contact.

Don: I didn't realize I did that. But come to think of it, you're right. I don't make good eye contact.

Critic: Your shirt is dirty.

Judy: No, it looks dirty, but actually that spot is a stain. I just washed this shirt.

Your critic: _____

Your response: _____

Clouding

Destructive, manipulative criticism with which you disagree deserves the assertive technique known as *clouding*. The manipulative critic takes a grain of truth and elaborates on it, using his or her ample imagination to put you down. An example would be, "Williams, you're late with that report? You're always late. I can't imagine how you keep your job with your inadequate work habits. Why, if everybody in this company were as slow and lazy as you, we'd have to install a bed in every office!"

The manipulative critic is an expert at name-calling and "you messages." This critic brings up old history and uses absolutes such as "always," "never," and "everyone." If you are foolish enough to try to reason with this critic, you only give him or her more ammunition. This critic is not interested in listening to you, even when asking you a direct question. This person's fragile ego requires being right and winning his or her points. When you hear manipulative criticism, use one of these three forms of clouding in response:

1. **Agree in part.** Find some part of the manipulative critic's statement that you think is true and agree with it. Rephrase the statement so that you can honestly concur. Drop the absolutes. Ignore the rest of the message. In response to the above example of criticism, if you were Williams, you might simply reply, "You're right, I am late with this report."

EXERCISE: RESPONDING TO CRITICISM IN PART

Recall a time when someone put you down. Respond to the part of the criticism with which you can agree and ignore the rest.

Criticism: _____

_____

Your response: _____

_____

2. **Agree in probability.** Find something in what the manipulative critic is saying with which you can probably agree. You can think to yourself, the odds of his being right are one in a hundred, as you reply, "You're probably right that I'm usually late." Change the critic's wording slightly so that you do not compromise your integrity and agree to something you don't believe.

EXERCISE: RESPONDING TO CRITICISM IN PROBABILITY

Recall a manipulative criticism directed at you and respond to the probability that there is truth in the criticism.

Criticism: _____

_____

Your response: _____

_____

3. **Agree in principle.** You can agree with the manipulative critic in principle. This involves simple logic: If X, then Y. "You're right. If everyone in the company were as slow and lazy as you say I am, the company would need to install beds in every office."

EXERCISE: RESPONDING TO CRITICISM BY AGREEING IN PRINCIPLE

Recall a manipulative criticism directed at you, and respond to the criticism in principle.

Criticism: _____

_____

Your response: _____

_____

Probing

Occasionally you will be uncertain about your critic's motivation. Is this critic trying to help you and is merely going about it awkwardly? Is this critic out to hurt you under the guise of being helpful? Are this critic's comments actually hiding unspoken beliefs, feelings, and desires? Especially if your critic is someone who matters to you, you may want to probe further into the criticism to answer these questions. This requires listening carefully, a major feat when someone is giving you criticism.

Here's an example if you were using probing in response to criticism from a coworker:

Coworker: Late again. Keeping banker's hours, are we?

You: What is it about my being late that bothers you?

Coworker: There's no such thing as a free lunch. You've been getting away with working less hard than the rest of us, and I'm mad!

You: What is it about your working harder than me that makes you mad?

Coworker: I haven't had a vacation in over a year, and I work overtime every night. At five o'clock, you're out of here. It's just not fair.

You: What is it about this lack of fairness that bothers you?

Coworker: Well, not that you've pinned me down, I don't believe there's such a thing as fairness. I guess I feel pretty stupid for working so hard when you're a living example that I don't have to. I should be taking better care of myself instead of getting on your case.

In this example, probing the critic was useful in placing responsibility for the dissatisfaction where it belonged, on the critic. Often, the critic won't budge from his position and is resistant to exploration.

EXERCISE: PRACTICE PROBING

The next time you are criticized and you are unsure whether the criticism is constructive or manipulative, use probing questions to respond to the criticism. Once you think you have clarified the motive behind the criticism, respond by acknowledging it or clouding it.

TAKING A STAND AND STICKING TO IT: THE BROKEN RECORD

Occasionally you encounter people—salesmen, children, or a stubborn friend—who will not take no for an answer. When you want to set limits and someone is having difficulty getting your message, you need to take a stand and stick to it, such as when your five-year-old wants to eat candy in the check-out line of the grocery store.

This approach is also effective in telling people what you want when their own motives are preventing them from seeing yours. An example would be if you were telling an uncooperative grocery clerk that you wanted to return the gallon of milk that had gone sour in the twenty-four hours since you bought it.

This approach involves five steps:

1. Choose carefully what you want or don't want. Review your perspective of the situation, your feelings, and your rights.

2. Create a brief, specific, easy-to-understand statement about what you want. One sentence is best. Give no excuses or explanations. Don't say "I can't." The other person will point out to you that this is just another excuse and show you how you can. It's much simpler and more truthful to say "I don't want to." Eliminate any loopholes in your brief statement that the other person could use to further his or her position.

3. Use body language to support your statement: good posture, direct eye contact, and a calm, confident, and determined voice.

4. Firmly repeat your brief statement as many times as necessary for the person to get your message and to realize that you won't change your mind. The other person will probably invent a number of reasons why you should. Eventually the reasons will run out, if you are persistent. Change your brief statement only if the other person finds a serious loophole in it.

5. You may choose to acknowledge the other person's opinions, feelings, or wants before returning to your broken record.

Here's an example of how this could work:

Boss: I hate to ask you to work Saturday after five days of overtime, but I have to because of our deadline.

You: I know the fiscal year ends next week, but I am not going to work Saturday.

Boss: I didn't think you were the kind of person who would let me down at a time like this. I really need your help.

You: I hear you are disappointed with me for not working this weekend, but I am not going to work Saturday.

Boss: If you don't do the work tomorrow, you'll have to cram it all in next week. You'll never get it all done!

You: I know that the work has to get done, and I am not going to work Saturday.

Boss: Well, I can't force you to come in, but you better be ready for some late nights next week!

You: Fine. See you next week.

EXERCISE: PRACTICE TAKING A STAND AND STICKING TO IT

Recall a time when you needed to set limits or ask for something from someone who was really stubborn. On a separate piece of paper, write down a dialogue in which you could respond, using this technique.

CONTENT-TO-PROCESS SHIFT

There are many times when the actual topic being discussed (the content) is less important than what is going on between you and another person (the process). For example, when you realize the conversation has been sidetracked, you may want to make a content-to-process shift: "Hey, we're talking about buying a new car when we both agreed we were going to discuss our bills." Or "Joking about this is taking us away from the task of solving this problem. As I was saying . . ."

When you think that another person's nonverbal communication is relevant, you can comment on it at that very moment: "I notice that you seem to not hear my requests until I raise my voice and look right in your face." Continuing with this example, you can use a content-to-process shift to share your feelings and thoughts: "I'm feeling frustrated and mad. I'm thinking that you are ignoring me and that feels disrespectful to me." When using a content-to-process shift, try to be a neutral observer rather than a critic.

Whatever the situation, remember to stand up for your legitimate rights by communicating assertively. Using the skills covered in this chapter, you can express your perspective, your feelings, and your wants and respond effectively to criticism and resistance.

CHAPTER 6

Fighting Fair: How to Disagree with Intimates

Fighting is inevitable in any intimate relationship. No two individuals are ever so compatible that they don't have conflicting desires, needs, and opinions. Unfortunately, it is all too easy to fall into the trap of unfair fighting, which often results in hurt, alienation, and unresolved differences. Whenever you are close to someone, you will have disagreements that can best be resolved by fair fighting.

Fair fighting is a clear, open discussion of your differences, without raising voices in anger or fists in violence. It follows a simple six-step outline that keeps the exchange respectful and peaceful, and maximizes your chances of arriving at a solution that is mutually agreeable.

The term *fair fighting* was coined by George Bach and Peter Wyden (1983) in *The Intimate Enemy*. This chapter teaches Bach's "fight for change" technique, modified with more recent cognitive behavioral strategies for anger management and joint conflict-resolution.

The advantages of fair fighting are simple and powerful:

■   You can get what you want and need in your intimate relationships.

■   You can avoid alienating your partner.

- You can handle conflict quickly and skillfully instead of avoiding it.

- You can have a deeper, more honest, and respectful intimate relationship.

MYTHS AND TRUTHS

Three commonly believed myths about conflict lead to unfair fighting—a harmful, unhealthy, ineffective way to resolve differences. Dispelling those myths and replacing them with three important truths about conflict paves the way to fair fighting.

The Myth	The Truth
Conflict is bad.	Conflict is normal.
I'm right; you're wrong.	We're both right.
Winner takes all.	Both win.

If you believe that "conflict is bad," then every disagreement represents a failure of the relationship. You start the process of conflict-resolution one down, doomed from the start. If you know that conflict is normal and inevitable, then disagreements are seen as part of the process of loving each other. Every conflict is a sign that the relationship is proceeding normally; it represents a new chance to change the relationship for the better.

The belief that "I'm right; you're wrong" is an immature, incomplete response to conflict. The mature, balanced truth is that we are both individuals with reasonable, understandable needs, desires, tastes, preferences, opinions, goals, and hopes. My need for stimulation and excitement may differ from your need for peace and quiet, but that doesn't mean that my needs are more important or legitimate than yours.

"Winner takes all" is a destructive myth that applies a narrow sports analogy to the entire universe of human interactions. It's a very rare conflict that allows for only one winner. Most times you can work together to find solutions that give each of you most of what you want, without depriving or exploiting the other. Both of you can win.

UNFAIR FIGHTING TACTICS

A number of tactics can be used in unfair fighting. Do any of the following seem familiar?

Bad Timing

One partner picks a fight at a time that isn't possible or convenient for the other. It's an unfair tactic to insist on talking about a problem when it's late, when one of you is tired, when you are rushing to get somewhere, or when you're working against an important deadline. Sometimes you might be in too public a space for a fight; you might be in heavy traffic or feeling sick. Fighting is not appropriate.

Avoidance

It is also an unfair tactic to avoid conflict by always claiming that the timing is bad: "It's too late to talk about this now . . . I have a headache . . . I can't deal with this until my dissertation is done . . . not while we're visiting my parents." If there is always a reason why one partner can't talk about a problem, it's avoidance.

Blaming

If you believe "I'm right; you're wrong," you tend to blame the other person for every problem. You may call the other person names, accuse him or her of lying or cheating or hating, induce guilt by bringing up past transgressions, assume hostile intentions, and exaggerate your differences. "You statements" abound and responsible "I statements" are rare.

Bringing Up Too Many Issues

When you are angry and attacking, or scared and defensive, you may tend to throw every rock you can lay your hands on. You may bring up every issue you can think of that shows how right you are and how wrong the other person is. It's an unfair fighting tactic to broaden the topic under discussion into a laundry list of the other person's faults.

Obscuring Feelings with Anger

Anger is usually the only feeling expressed in unfair fights. It obscures underlying quieter emotions, such as disappointment, jealousy, sadness, fear, loneliness, and so on. It's an unfair tactic to allow your anger to drown out other feelings that are more neutral and useful. In a fair fight, talking about your sadness or fear is often the doorway to resolution.

Demanding Vague Personality Changes

Demands that the other person be more "responsible," "caring," or "spontaneous"—these and other vague descriptions of personality traits, attitudes, or motivations—are forbidden in a fair fight. The vocabulary is too subjective, and making sweeping changes in your personality is too difficult and unlikely.

Making Threats

Excessive threats and ultimatums are tools of coercion that have no place in a fair fight. Threats such as "I'll leave you . . . I'll take the kids . . . I'll tell on you . . . I'll stop supporting you" are counterproductive because they are often unbelievable. They raise the stakes unnecessarily, escalating anger and blinding you to more reasonable solutions.

Escalation

Unfair fights tend to escalate. Escalation is not so much a tactic as it is a characteristic of unfair fighting. Unfair fights often move from quiet discussion to open disagreement, from vigorous debate to loud argument, from arguing to shouting, from yelling to breaking things, from destruction to throwing things, from throwing small things to hurling more and more dangerous things, from throwing to hitting.

Repetition

Unfair fights often recur. Like escalation, repetition is characteristic of unfair fighting. Unfair fights must be fought over and over again because they don't result in a mutually agreed upon and satisfying solution. Coming to the same dead end—anger, tears, silence, storming out—is a sign of unfair fighting. Unfair fights never end; they just lapse into a cease-fire until the next round.

EXERCISE: WHICH UNFAIR FIGHTING TACTIC WERE THEY USING?

Read the following scenarios. Fill in the blanks, identifying the unfair fighting tactic that each scenario illustrates.

1. Caitlin felt abandoned, jealous, and embarrassed as she watched her boyfriend Josh talking to the girl on the motorcycle. They were laughing and enthusing about the stupid machine while Caitlin stood around waiting for Josh to unlock their car. By the time they pulled out of the parking lot, Caitlin's feelings of abandonment, jealousy, and embarrassment had morphed into rage. In this scenario, Caitlan was _____

2. Cindy was tired after work. She had just an hour to get some dinner together, and then she had to take one kid to Girl Scouts and the other to a play rehearsal. And there was Jerry, complaining about the Mastercard bill, asking about her charges at Chez Joanne and Footloose, insisting on making up a monthly budget, while Cindy was trying to chisel the damn frozen ravioli apart. On Jerry's part, this was an example of _____

3. Carl was an okay husband, but Claire found him too practical and predictable. For their anniversary, he took her to dinner at the same old place, where he had made reservations two weeks earlier. During dessert he gave Claire her present: a new car vacuum. She started crying. In between sniffles and hiccups, she demanded that Carl be more romantic and spontaneous. Claire was guilty of _____

4. Whenever Jane talked to her dad about her exciting art classes, he would berate her for not studying something more practical. She would get defensive; he would get sarcastic. She'd call him a Philistine, and he'd call her a flake. She'd lapse into hurt silence, and he would finally apologize. They never settled anything, and the next "how's school?" talk would go the same way. Jane and her dad exhibited _____

5. When their mother died, Amy and Rachel had to divide her things. Amy had always resented her older sister, and late one night she went on a tirade, calling Rachel selfish, self-centered, unfair, snotty, and stuck up. Rachel countered by accusing Amy of sucking up to their parents and poisoning their Mom's mind against the rest of the family. Amy and Rachel were guilty of

_____

6. Joan's "family discussions" with Sebastian started calmly enough, but they always got out of hand. She would get shrill and start slapping the table for emphasis. Sebastian would start pacing around and interrupting her in a louder voice. Eventually she would run into the bathroom and slam the door. Sebastian would yell through the door, then storm out of the apartment and be gone for hours. Their family discussions are an example of _____

7. Jack wanted Ralph to get his art stuff off the kitchen table. They started arguing about who was the messier roommate, and Jack brought up the whole plaster-casting debacle, the way Ralph never separated the whites and the colors in the wash, his habit of leaving all the cupboard doors open, the state of his shoes and his car, his stinginess, and his obsession with cats. Jack was _____

8. Whenever Sue wanted to talk to Charlotte about their finances, she became frustrated. It was always too late or too early. Charlotte was too tired or had cramps or was just about to wash her hair. Charlotte had to wait for her bank statement to arrive, and then she couldn't find it. Then, when it turned up, she decided that what they really needed was the current Visa bill. Charlotte's behavior is an example of _____

9. If Jill pressed Roger too hard about his drinking or gambling, he said things like, "Listen, I'm under a lot of stress. I'm coping the best way I can in a tough situation. If you hassle me too, it just raises the stress level, and at some point I'm just out of here. I've had about all I can take and still hang in here." Roger was _____

Answers in sequence: obscuring feelings with anger; bad timing; demanding vague personality changes; repetition; blaming; escalation; bringing up too many issues; avoidance; making threats.

EXERCISE: ASSESSING YOUR UNFAIR TACTICS

In the spaces provided below, describe situations in which you have used these various tactics of unfair fighting. With whom did you use this tactic? When? What happened? Use extra paper if necessary to describe the situation.

Bad timing_____

_____

Avoidance_____

_____

Blaming _____

_____

Bringing up too many issues _____

_____

Obscuring feelings with anger _____

_____

Demanding vague personality changes _____

_____

Making threats _____

_____

Escalation _____

_____

Repetition _____

_____

RULES OF FAIR FIGHTING

Like most communication skills, fair fighting works best when both partners know the rules, and they follow them. Fighting with a skilled partner is like ballroom dancing or martial arts between two masters, an artistic, elegant, creative exchange that is both satisfying and effective.

However, the rules still work remarkably well when applied by only one partner. Fighting fair with an uninformed or unwilling partner is more work and less satisfying, but you will still get results. Also, your partner will pick up fair-fighting skills from your example, just as untrained singers and dancers benefit from performing with more experienced artists. Even if your partner resists the concept of fair fighting, you will still have the same advantage over your partner that the Tai Chi master has over the street brawler. So study the rules thoroughly, and follow them with care.

1. Set a time. Before you get into the topic, get your partner to agree that this is a good time to talk. Here are some examples of how to ask:

- "I'd like to talk about visiting my mother in the fall. Is this a good time?"

- "I have a bone to pick with you about the household chores. Do you have a minute?"

- "Let's sit down right now and figure out what to do about Jimmy, okay?"

If your partner is too tired or busy right now, make an appointment for later. You may have to be persistent. For example, Lilly didn't like the critical, nagging way her husband Peter talked to their son, Jeremy. But every time she brought up the topic, Peter avoided the issue by claiming to be too busy or tired. Finally, Lilly said, "I know you don't really want to talk about this, but I do. My feelings about how we interact with Jeremy are strong, and they're not going away. So if you can't talk now, when can I get your undivided attention?" Peter agreed to talk Saturday morning while Jeremy was at math tutoring.

2. State the problem in terms of facts and behavior. Describe what your partner does or doesn't do that bothers you. To avoid both blaming and demanding vague personality changes, stick to facts and behavior—observable actions or statements that are not open to interpretation:

- "The deadline for our workshop registration was last Monday and you haven't sent in the check yet."

- "The last time we had sex was six weeks ago, in Hawaii."

- "Today I got the third bounced check notice for this month."

In the past Lilly had nagged Peter for being too "critical" or "picky" or "impatient" with Jeremy. Her comments never made any difference in how he treated their son. Saturday morning she tried stating the problem more factually by focusing on one typical behavior: "Last Sunday you reminded Jeremy about his homework five or six times during the day. When he finished it late, after bedtime, you told him he was 'hopeless' and he went to bed crying."

3. Stick to one issue. Fight about one thing at a time. Resist the urge to drag in every mistake your partner has ever made. You are not a lawyer building a case by amassing overwhelming evidence. You are trying to change one behavior at a time, using a collaborative process. When your partner tries to distract you by bringing up your failings, remind him or her to stick to one issue:

- "I know there's lots of other things we don't agree on, but let's concentrate on this now."

- "I'd love to talk about my driving another time, but this is about Paul."

- "Let's stick to one subject at a time."

Lilly yearned to recite a long list of ways that Peter nagged and micromanaged Jeremy's studies, sports, and habits. It was especially difficult to stick to one issue when he said, "What about the way you're always losing your temper when he makes a mess in his room? That's worse than my concern over his grades." She said, "It's true I need to control my temper, but right now I want to talk about weekend homework, period."

4. Express all your feelings appropriately. Sure you feel angry, and you may have every right to feel that way. But it won't work to dump that anger on your partner. Express anger appropriately by using an "I statement" such as "I feel angry" or "I'm mad." Don't blame your partner for your anger by using "*you* statements," such as "You make me furious." Furthermore, include all the emotions you feel in addition to anger, such as depression, anxiety, jealousy, or guilt:

- "I feel sad and disappointed that things haven't worked out between us."

- "I'm worried about your health."

- "I'm afraid and lonely when I'm here by myself, and I don't know when you'll be back."

Lilly was angry at Peter, but, more important, she was worried about Jeremy's self-esteem under the onslaught of his father's criticism. She told Peter, "When I heard Jeremy crying in his room, I was so sad I felt like crying myself. I'm worried he will grow up really believing that he's stupid and hopeless."

5. Propose change. State what you want your partner to do or not do. Use clear, simple, unambiguous language that leaves no room for doubt or interpretation. Don't ask for an attitude change such as "Be more careful . . . considerate . . . forceful . . . creative." Phrase your proposed change in terms of behavior:

- "I want you to come home each weeknight by six thirty, or to call and tell me exactly when you'll be home."

- "I want us to go out to dinner or dancing or to a play once a month."

- "I want separate checking accounts and a clear list of who pays which bills."

Lilly told Peter exactly what she wanted him to say to Jeremy at Sunday breakfast: "Son, you're getting older now and I trust you to get your homework done on time and get to bed without me nagging you. I'll help if you ask me to, but otherwise I won't bug you about it. If you need to stay up late to finish, that's your business too."

6. Describe consequences. Ideally, describe positive, factual consequences that your partner will enjoy after making your proposed change: more money, fun, and free time. Better sex, health, and energy. Less stress, noise, and mess. Include emotional consequences such as how much closer and more harmonious your relationship will feel. As a last resort, include the negative consequences of failing to make your proposed change. But be careful to avoid threats and ultimatums. Make sure the negative consequences are realistic:

- "You need to start coming to bed by midnight. I can't continue to drag you out of bed and help you get to work on time."

- "If you retire, we can travel and play more golf. Otherwise, I'll take more golf trips with my friends."

Lilly predicted that without Peter's nagging, Jeremy would either finish his homework on time, late, or not at all. On time would be a boost to his self-esteem. Late would deprive him of sleep, motivate him to start earlier next week, and still boost his self-esteem. Not at all would prompt a note from the teacher, and they'd deal with it later. She offered to help Peter clean out the garage on Sunday to take his mind off Jeremy.

EXERCISE: PLANNING YOUR FAIR FIGHT SCRIPT

Use this exercise to plan how to discuss a problem with someone close. It will ensure that you follow the rules of fair fighting and maximize your chances of arriving at a mutually satisfactory solution. Choose a situation in which you've used unfair fighting tactics. This will give you an opportunity to fight fairly. Start with a minor problem, not the biggest issue in your life. Edit your script until it says just what you want to say, in your own style.

1. Set the time for the fight: _____

2. State the problem in terms of facts and behavior: _____

_____

_____

3. Express all your feelings appropriately: _____

_____

_____

4. Propose change: _____

_____

_____

5. State the positive consequences of change: _____

_____

_____

6. State any negative consequences of not changing: _____

_____

_____

Here is an example of how Sarah filled out her fair-fight script before talking to Daniel about getting a new computer:

1. **Set the time for the fight:** "I'd like to talk to you about my new computer. Is this a good time?"

2. **State the problem in terms of facts and behavior:** "I need a new computer. You have the ability to build me a custom system and install all sorts of fancy features and software that I don't really understand."

3. Express all your feelings appropriately: "I admire your knowledge, but I feel intimidated by it as well. Sometimes I feel overwhelmed by all the esoteric computer jargon. The thought of trying to understand the fine details that you love so much just depresses me."

4. Propose change: "This time I'd like to buy a plain vanilla system from a store, with only the bundled software that comes with the computer."

5. State the positive consequences of change: "That way I'll have a manual and a guarantee and access to support. I'll have a simple, common system that I have a hope of understanding. When I get stuck, I'll be able to find my own answers. I know that my computer won't be cool, but at least I'll understand it."

6. State any negative consequences. "If you build me a fancy system with no documentation, I'll be bugging you every time I can't remember how to do stuff. I'll feel dependent and resentful. You'll feel hassled and critical."

Before approaching the person you've chosen and trying out your script, read the rest of the chapter. This information will help you prevent escalation and prepare you for counter proposals.

PREVENTING ESCALATION

There are three things you can do to prevent escalation: watch nonverbal behavior, breathe deeply to slow the pace of the fight, and declare a time-out.

Monitor Nonverbal Behavior

First, be aware of your own and your partner's tones of voice. If voices get louder, that's a danger sign. Also watch for escalating body language: a shift from sitting to standing, pointing fingers, clenching fists, books slammed down, brandishing or throwing things, fast pacing, or shoving. When you start to notice these things, call for a time-out and cool down.

Breathe Deeply

When you notice that you are getting excited, consciously slow your breathing. Take deeper, slower breaths, inhaling deeply into your abdomen and releasing the air completely with a sigh. Suggest that your partner try it too. When you literally take a breather, it automatically calms your emotions and buys time.

Call a Time-Out

If breathing isn't enough, call a time-out. Agree ahead of time on a signal, such as a sports referee's T for time-out. There are specific rules for calling a time-out:

- No last words. As soon as one person calls time out, both stop talking.

- Leave immediately. The person who calls a time-out leaves the house or apartment, if possible, or at least goes into another room and closes the door. If you are in a car, just stop talking. A time-out should last about an hour.

- Always return when time is up.

- Don't use drugs or alcohol during the time-out.

- Try not to use the time-out to rehearse your argument. Use the time to get some physical exercise, or do something else to take your mind off the upsetting topic.

- Check in when you get back. Make sure you are both ready to resume. If not, make a date for the near future to finish the fight.

THE END OF A FAIR FIGHT

Sometimes a fight ends in simple agreement to your proposal for change. More often, your partner makes a counter proposal, you discuss it, and come up with a compromise solution.

Success depends on the fairness of the fight, not on the quality of the solution. Sometimes a fair fight ends with no agreement except to fight fairly again. That's all right. Many issues will take time and several discussions to resolve. Postponement is sometimes the only reasonable solution. The important thing is to agree on when you will take up the topic and fight again.

CHAPTER 7

Negotiating Conflict: Winning without Intimidating or Caving In

Everyone negotiates, not just diplomats, union leaders, and CEOs. You negotiate when you discuss repairs with your landlord, wages with your employer, or prices with a used-car salesperson. You negotiate whenever you and a relative stranger have conflicting desires yet must come to some sort of agreement. Negotiation allows you to get part of what you want without alienating others. Although both sides in a negotiation want to win, it is not in their interests to win at any cost, so the best solution is usually a mutually agreeable compromise.

Some people are poor negotiators because they hate and avoid conflict. They see all adversarial situations as no-win, lose/lose disasters, so they avoid confrontations in which they will have to negotiate for what they want. When they can no longer avoid a conflict and are forced into a negotiation, they perform poorly because they lack practice and a positive attitude. If you hate conflict, your first task is to adjust your attitude. Try to see conflict as an opportunity for positive change. Tell yourself, "Conflict is unavoidable. Negotiation is necessary."

Other people are poor negotiators because they are too soft or too hard in negotiations. Being too soft in a negotiation means not asking clearly for what you really want and giving up too soon. Your adversary might think kindly of you, but you won't get what you want. Being too hard in a negotiation means taking a position and refusing to budge. Your adversary will hate you, and you still won't get what you want.

Like Goldilocks in the Three Bears' house, you should seek a middle ground that is neither too soft nor too hard, but just right. When you negotiate just right, both sides keep their dignity and each side gets part of what it wants.

The techniques of *just right* negotiation will work whether you are dealing with one other person, such as your boss, or with a group of people, such as the building permit department or a homeowners association. Adding more personalities to a conflict can complicate the process, but the principles of negotiation remain the same.

STEPS OF "JUST RIGHT" NEGOTIATION

In another sense, just right negotiation is also both *just* and *right*. It is just to objectively consider both sides of a conflict, and it is right to want both sides to prosper. Just right negotiation has four stages: preparation, discussion, proposition, and resolution.

Preparation

Before you confront the other side, you need to determine three options:

- your ideal outcome

- a pretty good fall-back position

- the worst deal you would accept

This marks the boundaries of the territory in which it will be comfortable and beneficial for you to negotiate. For example, if you want your apartment painted, you might decide on these three options:

- Ideal: *I pick different colors for each room; the landlord pays for paint and professional painters.*

- What's acceptable: *I pick one color for all the rooms, the landlord buys paint, and his handyman does the painting.*

- Worst acceptable deal: *landlord picks color and buys paint; I do the painting.*

Preparation also includes research: doing your homework to support your position, learning about your opponent's interests, and finding out about how others have solved similar problems. During breaks in a negotiation, you will return to the preparation stage to refine your options, look up additional information, talk to other people, and brainstorm creative propositions.

Discussion

This is the heart of negotiation. You and your opponent describe the facts of the matter, your emotions, and your opinions. You might say to your landlord, "My apartment hasn't been painted since I moved in eight years ago. When I'm in the bathroom or the kitchen I feel particularly dark and depressed, they're so dingy. I think it's time to paint the apartment."

In a negotiation, you take turns describing the situation. You each do this in terms of your own needs and interests. Discussion takes place throughout a negotiation, as you resolve deadlocks by repeatedly explaining your own viewpoint and asking for more information about the other person's position.

Proposition

To resolve the conflict, you make a proposition. A good place to start is with your ideal outcome: "I'd like to pick a nice set of colors and have you pay Diamond Painting to come in and do the job while I'm on vacation next month."

Your adversary then makes a counter proposition: "I admit your apartment needs painting, but I can't afford Diamond's prices for a custom job. I have gallons of antique white on hand, if you're interested in painting it yourself."

You may discuss both propositions and take a time out to think about it. Eventually you alter your original proposition, perhaps with a version of your "acceptable" option. The other person proposes something else, and gradually, with more discussion, you arrive at a mutually agreeable proposition near the middle ground.

Resolution

If you arrive at a mutually acceptable proposition, you agree on it, and the negotiation is successfully resolved. For example, your landlord might agree to pay his handyman to paint most rooms antique white and to buy a custom color for the bathroom.

Sometimes the resolution step ends in disagreement. You do not reach a mutually agreeable proposition, so you resolve to negotiate again later. Each party returns to the preparation step to do some creative brainstorming, and the negotiation process starts over.

EXERCISE: WITH WHOM DO YOU NEED TO NEGOTIATE?

List at least three people or groups of people with whom you need to negotiate, and then identify the conflict that you need to negotiate with each one.

Person or Group   **Conflict**

1. _____   _____

2. _____   _____

3. _____   _____

4. _____   _____

HOW TO DO JUST RIGHT NEGOTIATION

Conflicts become hostile when people lock themselves into one position and become identified with that position. They experience any criticism of their position as a personal attack.

Don't Take It Personally

The first rule of successful negotiation is to remove your ego from the discussion. Don't lock yourself into a single possible solution. Go into the discussion with the attitude that you have plenty of options and that there is a wide variety of possible solutions, many of which can be acceptable to both parties. Assume that both of you are reasonable people, with many legitimate, overlapping interests, and you can reach a fair solution to the problem at hand.

For example, don't call your neighbor an insensitive creep for running his leaf blower at six thirty Sunday morning. Instead say, "I appreciate how hard you work to keep your yard up. It makes the whole neighborhood look better. But I like to sleep in on Sundays. Could you hold off on the leaf blowing until after nine?"

Put Yourself in the Other Person's Shoes

Empathy will take you further than endless strategizing, one-upmanship, and clever tricks. Put yourself in your adversary's shoes and ask yourself, "What does this person want? How does this person feel? What is fair from his or her point of view? What does he or she need to feel good about a solution?"

Remember to offer feedback, to paraphrase and express what other people *feel, think,* and *need.* For example, you might say to a prospective employer, "I can understand that you might *feel* nervous hiring a younger person for this position, that you might *think* an older person would have more experience dealing with people. I know you *need* someone who can take responsibility from day one." Feeding back information shows that you have heard the other side, that you respect the other person and take him or her seriously, and that you are a reasonable, fair negotiator.

Likewise, you should give your adversaries a chance to understand your side, by using the same *think, feel, need* approach: "I *feel* very excited about the challenge of this position, and I *think* I have more enthusiasm for the job than an older person might. All I *need* is a chance to prove myself. I'd like to try it for a month and prove to you that I can do it."

EXERCISE: SUMMARIZING THE OTHER SIDE'S POSITION

Pick one person with whom you are in conflict and summarize that person's position in the space below, according to what he or she thinks, feels, or needs:

_____   thinks _____

_____

_____

_____ feels _____

_____

_____

_____ needs _____

_____

_____

Define Conflict in Terms of Common Interests

In every conflict under negotiation, there are common interests that keep bringing both parties back to the discussion. You will never read in the newspaper that talks between the teachers union and the school district have been broken off forever, that the teachers have all decided to become postal employees and the school board will open a savings and loan. That will never happen because both sides have a strong, common interest in education that draws them back to the bargaining table until a mutually acceptable resolution is hammered out.

Rather than outlining the competing demands and positions that separate you and your opponent, look for the underlying common interests that connect you. After you find out what your opponent wants, your next question should be, "Why do you want that?" For example, you might ask a prospective employer, "Why do you want me to work alone here after dark?" You may find out that there is a special customer who only comes in late at night, or that the person who had the job for years preferred night hours, or that the business owner just likes to see the store lit up at night. You both have a common interest in running a profitable store. When you know the interests behind the other person's position, you can propose changes that will satisfy those interests and still get you home before dark: making a sales call on the special customer on your way home, finding another clerk who wouldn't mind covering late hours, or just leaving the lights on a timer.

Remember that many interests are emotional in nature and cannot be reduced to dollars and cents. People often want your respect and their own self-esteem more than they want the $300 you are haggling over. They don't want to give in on that $300 because they don't want to "lose" or look weak or incompetent. If you suspect that this is the case, describe your proposition not in terms of money but in terms of how generous and wise your opponent would be to compromise with you.

Be patient. Don't blurt out your preconceived solution in the first five minutes. Take the time necessary to tease out mutual interests and put them into words. For example, if you are trying to save money when hiring a dance hall for your favorite charity's dance, you might say: "I can see that you take a lot of pride in your facility and want to host only quality events here. We also want our dance to be remembered as the best ever. I can see how a $1,500 cleaning fee and a million dollar insurance rider helps you keep your standards up. That's why you are our first choice for a venue, because it's such a nice, well-maintained, and well-run facility. Your reputation will make it easier for us to sell tickets." Here's how you might diagram the different interests in this negotiation and where interests overlap.

Nonprofit Dance Sponsor's Interests	Dance Hall's Interests
Make money for cause	Maximize revenue
Keep expenses down	Reduce liability risk
Sell lots of tickets	Keep hall clean
Serve community	Be a community resource
Reduce liability risk	Insure against damages
Become an annual event	Guarantee future business

Some of these interests are in direct opposition, such as the nonprofit's desire to keep expenses down and the dance hall's desire to maximize revenue. But they share many interests: reducing liability, serving their community, and developing a long-term relationship.

EXERCISE: WHAT ARE YOUR COMMON INTERESTS?

Think about someone with whom you are having a conflict. In the two columns below, list your interests and your opponent's interests. Draw lines to connect your common interests.

Your Interests   **Your Opponent's Interests**

_____   _____

_____   _____

_____   _____

_____   _____

_____   _____

Brainstorm Numerous Options

Remember the appropriate attitude: there are many agreeable options to resolve any conflict. Let go of your favorite solution and the idea that you must get the largest slice of pie. Remind yourself that some pie is better than no pie, and that there may be a way to make the whole pie bigger.

Remember to do your homework: find out the going rate, usual benefit package, average rent, typical wage, price of similar items, or whatever you need to know, so you are well-informed as you go into the negotiation.

At this point, if possible, you can hold a brainstorming session with the people you know who are on your side of the conflict, and any advisors or interested parties who you think might have good ideas. A group of five to eight people is ideal. Pick someone to be the leader and keep you on track. That person should explain the rules of brainstorming:

- Criticism is forbidden.

- The more ideas the better, no matter how bizarre.

- The session is off the record.

- Ideas won't be attributed to the individuals suggesting them.

Come up with a large list of ideas. Write down everything and discuss or criticize nothing. Examine the problem from all angles. When the flow of ideas stops, the freewheeling part of the session is over.

Now you can analyze and criticize. Underline the good ideas. Develop pretty good ideas into better ones. Combine two good ideas into one great idea. You should end up with a list of several ideas, each of which could be an acceptable option for solving your problem.

If you don't have the luxury of partners to brainstorm with, do it on your own. Imagine viewing the problem from different points of view. How would a lawyer, a priest, a scientist, your mom, an accountant, or a judge solve this problem?

Consider the classic compromise strategies that even children understand: You pour the soda, and I'll choose which glass I want. Consider assigning values to disputed property and dividing it down the middle. When negotiating a fee, consider splitting the difference or trading time for money by setting up payment over time.

If you think that some of your options may be too hard for your opponent to accept, consider classic ways of softening propositions: instead of proposing a permanent change, suggest a trial period and future evaluation. Propose partial rather than sweeping changes. For example, set a limit on the expenses you want your opponent to pay for. Say that the terms of your agreement will be in force for a limited time. Make unconditional demands conditional. Make binding decisions nonbinding.

Rank your options into three rough categories: your ideal solution, a pretty good solution, and the worst deal you will accept.

Lucinda's daughter was going off to college, and Lucinda needed more money. She needed a 15 percent raise to make ends meet, but no one at her work was getting more than 5 percent because the economy was in a slump. After brainstorming with her daughter, her mother, and her best friends, she had a long list of ideas. She crossed out embezzlement, blackmail, and being promoted to CEO as either too illegal or unlikely. But that left her with a sizable list of options:

- *Explain my financial situation.*

- *Get promoted or transferred to a better paying position within the same company.*

- *Work longer hours or the night shift.*

- *Ask for money-saving fringe benefits: company car, home computer, clothing allowance.*

Lucinda imagined her problem from the point of view of her boss and the personnel manager. She realized that they would not be impressed by her financial crisis. The only reasons they ever gave raises were for increases in average cost-of-living, productivity, profitability, or responsibility. Therefore she added to her list of options:

- *Point out that my expenses were under budget last year, and my productivity has increased.*

- *Ask for more responsibility.*

■   *Volunteer to create a special clearance sales program for obsolete stock.*

To soften her propositions, Louise planned to ask that her 15 percent raise be phased in over three quarters, and she made it contingent on increased productivity, responsibility, and profitability.

Finally, Louise ranked her options in three categories:

Ideal solution: *Justify 15 percent by pointing out my budget and productivity numbers.*

Pretty good: *Justify 15 percent by asking for more responsibility, such as a promotion, a transfer, and so on. Or volunteer to set up clearance sale program.*

Worst deal: *Take 10 percent plus better fringe benefits but with increased responsibility (see above).*

EXERCISE: BRAINSTORMING OPTIONS

With a group of your constituents and friends, or by yourself, brainstorm at least ten options for solving the conflict you have been working with:

1. _____

2. _____

3. _____

4. _____

5. _____

6. _____

7. _____

8. _____

9. _____

10. _____

Cross out the illegal, unlikely, insane, or otherwise unacceptable options. Circle the best ones. Combine and improve upon your better ideas to try to come up with four or five distinctly different and agreeable options.

Turn Options into Propositions

At this point in a negotiation, you've opened a clear, calm, mutually respectful channel of communication with your opponent. You have stated the problem in terms of your common interests and have explored your differing interests so that both of you understands each other. You have privately brainstormed a list of acceptable options. It's time to make a proposition.

Start with your ideal solution. Begin describing it slowly in terms that make it a turn-on rather than a turnoff for your opponent. How you phrase your proposition makes a huge difference in whether your opponent finds it agreeable or disagreeable. Turn-ons take your opponent's interests into account. They show how your proposition will be good for the other person. Turn-ons are often couched in terms of a choice or an implied compromise. Turn-offs are based on your needs alone and alienate the other person. Here are some sample turnoffs:

- "You better fix the roof right away or I'm moving out."

- "I can't go a penny over $5,000 for a car with this much mileage. That's my last and final offer."

- "I've got to have the estimate before the end of April and the whole job done no later than June first."

The same solutions can be stated as turn-ons:

- "The leaks in the roof have already discolored the ceiling in the living room. I'm afraid the next big storm will ruin all the plaster. Would you rather fix the roof and paint the ceiling right now, or wait until I leave for vacation?"

- "This is a very solid car, maybe a better one than I can afford. You've taken good care of it, and eventually you might be able to get more for it than I can offer. However, I have $5,000 in cash that I can pay you today, no waiting."

- "If I give you until June first to finish the work, can you get me an estimate by March first?"

EXERCISE: MAKING AGREEABLE PROPOSITIONS

From your list of options that you brainstormed in the last exercise, write three propositions that are agreeable turn-ons.

_____

_____

_____

WHEN THE GOING GETS TOUGH

It would be nice if every negotiation went smoothly and your adversaries rolled over like friendly puppy dogs. But it isn't likely. Sometimes you have to deal with big dogs, mean dogs, or dirty dogs.

When Big Dogs Have All the Power

Sometimes you will have to negotiate with a boss, a building inspector, a tax auditor, a bankruptcy judge, a cop, or someone else who simply has way more power than you have. In this case, you have to be realistic about your chances of winning. You may very well lose, and you have to be prepared for that.

Start by figuring out your best alternative to a negotiated solution. For example, if you don't get the raise you want, you can quit. If you are actually willing to risk this alternative, and your opponent has shot down your other options, you can use it as a threat: "If you can't see your way clear to giving me what I deserve, I'm going to have to quit and look elsewhere."

Other times, there is no strong alternative to negotiation and you should not threaten. On the contrary, you should calmly, coolly outline the facts of the matter, and not lose your temper. To do this, you have to spend extra time in preparation, doing your homework and calming yourself. When you start the negotiation, appeal to your opponent's sense of fairness and hope for the best.

Say you would like to have all the classes at your previous college counted towards your new major at your new college, even though the requirements and class content differ somewhat. Don't go into the administration office thinking that you are a lone warrior about to do battle with a rigid bureaucratic ogre. Let go of the idea that you must defend every last credit to the death. Tell yourself that you have many good options for taking interesting classes without repeating boring prerequisites. Realize that the woman behind the desk has nothing against you personally. She wants you to get a good education, without repeating material you have already mastered. However, she also has a legitimate interest in protecting the college's accreditation and the integrity of its degree programs. Organize your records carefully and make sure you fully understand the requirements you must complete. Then calmly throw yourself on the mercy of the court.

Sometimes sheer numbers can bolster a weak position. Despite the inherent greed and exploitation of capitalism, the labor movement has wrested better pay and working conditions from management over the years through collective bargaining. Are there others in your position? Can you drum up support for a group effort to effect change in the face of opposition from the powers that be? It's worth a try. See chapter 17 on public speaking.

When Mean Dogs Won't Play Nice

Sometimes there isn't a power imbalance, but your opponent makes negotiation difficult by a hostile attitude or by a refusal to compromise from an entrenched position. When this happens, you can try one of several tactics:

Persistent Questioning

When your opponent takes a position and won't budge an inch, ask "Why?" When they give an evasive nonanswer, use it as the basis of another "why" question. Repeat the process until you get to your opponent's real interest in the matter. Persistent questioning is how three-year-olds drive their parents crazy. In the hands of a skillful adult negotiator, persistent questioning is a way of breaking through an entrenched position to uncover the interests hidden underneath. Here's how it goes:

You: Why won't you even consider a flextime policy?

Boss: Because it's against company policy.

You: Why is it against company policy?

Boss: Because it's unworkable.

You: Why is it unworkable?

Boss: Because there's no accountability.

You: Why is there no accountability?

Boss: Because we don't have time clocks.

You: Why don't we have time clocks?

Boss: They're too expensive.

You: How much do they cost?

Boss: We don't know.

You: Let's find out.

Redirection

Other times your opponent won't answer your question but spends all the time attacking your position. When this happens, resist the impulse to dig in and defend your position. Instead, use a tactic that deflects the attacks and redirects the discussion. Say things like, "That's very interesting. What else is wrong with my position? How would you alter it to make it more acceptable to you?" By enlisting your opponent in brainstorming your own options, you dodge the attack and get your opponent to generate counter propositions.

Reframing Personal Attacks

If your opponent attacks you personally, reframe his or her words as an attack on the problem, not on you. For example, if your landlord blames you for "stirring up trouble in the building, meddling in everyone else's affairs, and getting the tenants all upset," respond by saying, "Yes, you're right. Most of your tenants are upset and excited about making some changes to improve the building." Resist the impulse to respond in kind. An exchange of insults is not a negotiation. Refusing to take your opponent's attack personally redirects his or her attention to the issues.

Using the One-Text Procedure

If both of you are so antagonistic and entrenched in your positions that open negotiation is impossible, you might try a mediation technique called the *one-text procedure*. A neutral third party is selected to interview both sides, and then draw up a single text that outlines a compromise solution. Both of you critique the text. Then the neutral third party revises and resubmits it. With this procedure, the two sides never meet face to face. Over many revisions, they may finally agree on one text. This is how the United States mediated the Camp David agreement between Egypt and Israel. The text went through twenty-one drafts.

When Dirty Dogs Pull Dirty Tricks

Sometimes your opponent is not only entrenched but is also willing to use dirty tricks, such as lies, deception, intimidation, bribery, or blackmail. Sometimes such tricks are childishly simple ones, such as seating you with the sun in your eyes or in short chairs at a conference table. Whatever the dirty trick, you should respond by calling process and negotiating for fair play.

Calling process means that you stop talking about the topic under negotiation and start talking about the process that is going on at the moment. For example, "Before we get started, I'd like to mention that my copy of the contract is very faint and that the sun is in my eyes. I'd like the blinds lowered and a clear copy."

While you have the floor, negotiate for fair play by outlining the principles of just right negotiation:

- Each party must negotiate fairly, in good faith.

- You are an honest person, open to reason, and expect the same of the other party.

- You believe many viable options must exist that can be mutually agreeable.

- Both of you have legitimate interests, many of which are shared.

- You're willing to listen to the other party explain his or her interests, and you expect the same courtesy.

- You want the other party to agree to proceed in a civilized manner.

Most often this will work and you can continue to negotiate on a more level field. If you can't get agreement to the concept of just right negotiation, you should consider bringing in a mediator, initiating a lawsuit, or giving up the idea of making a deal with your opponent.

Sometimes your opponent wants conflict more than he or she wants resolution, and negotiation is impossible. For instance, union negotiators may purposely drag out bargaining until a strike deadline is closer. Environmental activists may want publicity more than the cleanup of a particular toxic site.

Always Leave the Door Open to Future Negotiation

If you must give in and accept a bad deal, or break off negotiation entirely with a big dog, mean dog, or dirty dog, don't slam the door on your way out. Resist the urge to blame, call names, threaten, yell, and stomp away. Don't call a press conference to smear the other side or begin badmouthing your opponent to all your friends and acquaintances.

Always leave the door open to future negotiations because conditions tend to change over time. Petty bureaucrats retire, nasty landlords sell their properties, the filthy rich take a bath in the stock market, and the powerful lose their mandate as political winds shift. Try to part with this kind of language: "I'm sorry we haven't been able to come to a mutually agreeable resolution, but I won't give up hope. Even though we're stymied for the time being, I don't consider the issue completely closed. I still think there are common interests between us that will require us to talk more about this in the future. I intend to stay in touch, stay informed, and stay open to discussion."

Follow up by occasional emails, phone calls, or other forms of communication, maintaining a neutral tone. Use these contacts to gently keep the door open and remind your opponent that you are still interested in mutually advantageous change.

CHAPTER 8

Holding Your Own: Coping with Differences in Power

When you are one down in an uneven relationship it's important to speak up for yourself. Learning to speak up will help you

- take care of yourself when you are in a subordinate position

- move toward a more egalitarian peer relationship when you have been giving away your power

- improve your self-esteem

Power is the ability to make others think, behave, and feel the way you want them to. When you are in a relationship in which someone has power over you, they are in a position to affect your well-being. Why would you be in a relationship where you are in a one-down position? Someone may have official power over you because of their title or position. When you were a kid, you were subordinate to your parents, coaches, minister, doctor, and teachers. As you grew older, you entered into subordinate relationships with professors, bosses, supervisors, superior officers, and senior partners.

The other reason you might be in a one-down position in a relationship is that you are not using the power that you have. You might be a talented, attractive, hard-working, successful, good person, and yet, for some reason, you tend to act submissive. You may do this in just one relationship and only some of the time, such as with a critical parent, a threatening mate or an overbearing boss, or you may do it in all your relationships. You do it by allowing others to make decisions for you, and by deferring to their opinions and actions rather than asserting your own. You do it by allowing them to breach a personal boundary that is part of how you define who you are and what is important to you (Katharine 2000).

PROTECTING YOUR PERSONAL BOUNDARIES

A personal boundary may be physical, sexual, intellectual, or emotional. When someone touches you in a way that you do not like or makes disrespectful comments about how you appear, that is a physical boundary violation. People are violating your boundaries when they put your ideas down or when they belittle your feelings. Boundary violations occur whenever others knowingly or unintentionally cross your comfort zone.

Boundary violations can be corrected immediately, but both parties must do something. First, if you have been offended, you need to let the other person know of the offense. Second, the offender must respond respectfully. This usually takes the form of an apology or some expression of concern about the violation. When someone offends you and you don't tell them, you allow yourself to be victimized and you give away a piece of yourself.

Boundary violations occur frequently. In the pursuit of their own self-interests, people often say or do things that are offensive. If you tend to be passive and not express your thoughts, feelings, and needs, people may never know that they have violated one of your boundaries. It is in the process of speaking up for yourself that you train others to treat you the way you want to be treated. While other people may not always agree with you, at least you will have been true to yourself by making an effort to take care of yourself.

There are a variety of reasons for why some people are more submissive than others. If, when you were a child, adults did not support your efforts to stand up for your own perceptions, opinions, feelings, and wants, you are unlikely to have developed a good sense of who you are. In this case, you would have difficulty defining and defending your own boundaries. If powerful people violated your boundaries, you are likely to have shame and confusion about your boundaries and your right to protect them. This would be a good time to review your legitimate rights in chapter 5. Remember, children's boundaries are often violated, and you need to recognize your rights as an adult. You can learn to create and protect healthy boundaries in the here and now by paying attention to your perceptions, opinions, feelings, and wants, and by practicing asserting them.

EXERCISE: WITH WHOM ARE YOU IN A ONE-DOWN RELATIONSHIP?

Give some thought to your significant relationships, the ones that are on-going and matter to you. Who has official power over you because of their title or position of authority? With whom are you in a one-down relationship because you have tended to give this person your power by not speaking up for yourself effectively?

List the people with whom you are in a one-down position. Check whether your underdog status is due to the fact that they are in a position of authority over you (legitimate power) or due to your giving away your power to them (submission) or both. If there are many people in the same category, such as "any woman I date," just list that category.

Angie, an office manager in a small engineering firm, wrote out the following list for herself:

Name and Relationship	Legitimate power	Submission
Mr. Barker (boss)	X	X
Ms. Tomas (voice teacher)	X	
Engineers on staff		X
Roy (boyfriend)		X
Dad		X
Sylvia (big sister)		X
Landlord	X	

She had initially listed her father as having legitimate power over her. She changed her mind, since she hadn't lived with him in years. Any power he had over her, she realized, was power she gave him.

Now you give it a try.

Name and Relationship	Legitimate power	Submission

WHY ARE YOU IN A ONE-DOWN RELATIONSHIP?

One reason you might be in a subordinate position to another person is that you think he or she has some special knowledge or expertise that you lack. As a result, you defer to this person's opinion in some significant area of your life rather than figure things out on your own. For instance, you may rely on a mate to be your financial planner and manage your money, or your engineer father to fix mechanical things for you, or your friends to plan your social activities. When others make the decisions or do things for you in a significant area of your life, you are at risk of underfunctioning in that area. You lose confidence in taking care of yourself in that area because you don't get the experience necessary to be skillful. This becomes a problem when you don't like what others are doing or the way they are treating you. Perhaps they subtly put you down for being less skillful than they are. You may end up tolerating abuse because you lack the self-confidence to take charge of this area of your life.

Another reason you might be in a one-down relationship is because you simply like certain aspects of being associated with that other person that you don't want to lose: great sex, love, approval, happiness, financial security, status, or companionship. You may believe, rightfully or not, that in order to be with a particular person, you must sacrifice valuable aspects of yourself. Rather than risk someone's disapproval or even end the relationship, you may stop working outside the home, spending time with friends or your own family, pursuing your creativity, or being too outspoken or too free.

You might be in a subservient relationship because you fear you will be punished if you assert your rights to be an equal. Traditionally, men have used coercion to keep women in their place. Many contemporary women still do as their men tell them because they fear they will be battered or end up economically disadvantaged if they don't.

Of course, there are many subtle ways that one person can punish another. It may be more pleasant to hand over the remote to the TV set rather than put up with a sulky partner for the evening. It may be easier to do the yard work, even though you would rather watch the game, than to endure your partner's complaints. It may be safer not to invite your friends or family over for dinner and live the life of a semi-recluse rather than to risk your partner blowing up or saying something really obnoxious. Each time you give in to another person to avoid a painful encounter, you are giving up a bit of yourself.

EXERCISE: DEVELOPING AWARENESS OF HOW AND WHY YOU GIVE YOUR POWER AWAY

For the next week, keep a log in which you record each time you give away your power. An example might be when someone violates one of your boundaries and you don't let them know about it. Another example would be when you do something you would rather not do, or you don't do something that is important to you, because you are afraid of negative repercussions from someone you have a relationship with. These are unpleasant events that you will prefer to forget about as quickly as possible, so it is important to write them down at once, if only in a few words to jog your memory later when you have time to examine what happened and why. At the end of each day, complete your log for that day. Who violated what boundary by doing what, and why did you let him or her get away with it?

Angie, the office manager, wrote the following in her log:

Day	Angie's Examples of Giving Power Away	Why?
Monday	Allowing Frank, one of the engineers I support, to tell me how to conduct my personal life.	He reminds me of my dad, and I respect his opinion. I want his approval.
Tuesday	Letting Louis, another engineer, get away with crude comments about my body and what I am wearing.	I'm too embarrassed. I don't want to make a scene. I don't want to hurt his feelings or get him in trouble.
Wednesday	I let my boss take advantage of me by not saying no to too much work. I end up working nights and weekends without pay.	I want his approval, a raise, and a fat bonus.
Thursday	Not telling my sister that I don't appreciate her comments about my weight problem.	Pride. I tell myself I should have better self-control and I deserve criticism.
Friday	Having sex with my boyfriend when I don't feel like it.	Fear of losing him.

Now it's your turn. Use extra paper if necessary.

Day	Examples of Giving Your Power Away	Why?
Monday		
Tuesday		
Wednesday		
Thursday		
Friday		
Saturday		
Sunday		

CONSIDER YOUR OPTIONS

Now that you have identified how you give your power away and why, consider whether it is worth your while to change how you communicate with these people, and, if so, how will you go about doing it? To answer this question, you can do an exercise, adapted from Black and Enns (1997). Here's how Angie did the exercise.

Angie's example:

Situation 1: "Allowing Frank to make important decisions about my personal life when I could be making them myself."

What is bad about letting this continue? "I am allowing my intellectual and emotional boundaries to be violated. I'll become too dependent on him. I'll resent him and be mad at myself for not learning how to make these decisions myself."

What good can come from changing this situation? "I will become independent. I will become skillful at making my own decisions and develop self-confidence. I'll have better self-esteem."

Healthy options: "Tell Frank that, as much as I have appreciated his sound advice and fatherly concern, I see myself becoming too dependent on him rather than growing up and learning to take care of myself. I want to start making decisions about my personal life on my own, without his input. Until I learn how to do this, I want to limit my relationship with him to professional topics only."

Situation 2: "Inappropriate sexual advances at work from Louis."

What is bad about letting this continue? "I'll continue to feel degraded and pissed off. I never know what he is going to say or do next, so I'm on my guard when I have to deal with him. I've started questioning what it is about me that would make this man treat me this way, as if there were something wrong with me, not him. I'm distracted from my work."

What good can come from changing this situation? "Self-respect, peace of mind, normal work relationships, and better concentration."

Healthy options: "I have read a pamphlet on workplace sexual harassment, so I know my rights. I want to tell Louis that I think that he is sexually harassing me, give him specific examples of his behavior that I consider forms of sexual harassment, let him know that I find this kind of behavior really offensive, and tell him to stop or I will have to report him to our boss. I can also give him the pamphlet."

Situation 3: "Allowing my boss to give me so much work that I am working excessive overtime."

What is bad about letting this continue? "Job burnout! I'm irritable. I'm having more frequent headaches, my concentration is poor, so I'm making more mistakes. By the time I get home, I don't have time or energy to exercise or socialize, and I eat junk food. I probably will end up quitting or get fired."

What good can come from changing this situation? "I will be a more relaxed, happy, healthy, productive worker, and I can get my personal life back on track."

Healthy options: "I can make a list of my current responsibilities and take them to my boss, explaining to him how much time each responsibility takes. I can tell him I am no longer willing to work overtime because it is negatively affecting my performance, as well as my health and personal life. I can ask him to prioritize my responsibilities so that during an eight-hour day I can concentrate on what he considers the most important items. I can train an assistant to help me. With his authorization, I can give back some of my responsibilities to the engineers I support. If all else fails, I can look for another job."

Situation 4: "My sister making snide comments about my weight."

What is bad about letting this continue? "She's violating my physical and emotional boundaries. It feeds my guilt and low self-esteem. I resent my sister and I loathe myself."

What good can come from changing this situation? "Improved self-esteem. Honest, open relationship with my sister."

Healthy options: "I can self-disclose to my sister that her criticisms only make me feel worse about myself, and ask her to focus on what she likes about me, rather than what she detests."

Situation 5: "Having sex with my boyfriend when I don't want to."

What is bad about letting this continue? "By not leveling with him, I am letting him violate my sexual and emotional boundaries. I'm ignoring my own feelings and needs. I'm enjoying sex less, and I'm starting to resent my boyfriend for being so demanding."

What good can come from changing this situation? "I can acknowledge and take care of my own feelings and needs. I can improve our sex by doing it only when we both want it. I can improve our relationship by being honest."

Healthy options: "I can level with my boyfriend about how I'm experiencing our sexual relations and what I would like."

EXERCISE: WHAT ARE YOUR OPTIONS?

For each person with whom you are in a one-down relationship, describe the situation, what's bad about letting it continue, what good could result from changing the situation, and your options. Use extra paper, as necessary, to describe each situation.

Situation: _____

_____

What is bad about letting this continue? _____

_____

_____

What good can come from changing this situation? _____

_____

_____

Healthy options: _____

_____

_____

SPEAKING UP

Now that you have examined the situations in which you have difficulty defending your boundaries, you are ready to exercise your healthy options for change. You will be able to use the communication skills you have learned thus far in this book.

Addressing a Long-Term Problem

For situations that involve an on-going problem, prepare ahead of time to talk to the other person. Think about what you want to say, as well as responses to what you anticipate the other person will say. Then ask the other person when would be a good time to talk about it. Angie did this with her boss in the following example:

Angie: Mr. Barker, I'd like to set up a time to go over my responsibilities for the purpose of reorganizing my work so that I can be more effective as an office manager.

Boss: Right now is fine. Someone just canceled an appointment with me.

Angie: The problem, as I see it, is that I have too much work to do in an eight-hour day. I'm sure you're not aware of how much overtime I'm working, since I take care of pay roll, but it's too much. It's not economical for the company, and I need to cut back for my health and personal life.

Boss: You're right, Angie, I trust you. I figure that as long as the job gets done, it's okay with me.

Angie: I appreciate that I have your trust and confidence. Here is a list of my responsibilities and how much time each of them takes. I'd like you to look the list over and tell me which are most important to you to get done. That way, at the end of eight hours, I will have handled what you consider a priority. The rest will just have to wait.

Boss: (after looking over the list) It looks like I need to clone you in order to get all of the things I consider a priority done.

Angie: That, or hire me an assistant.

Boss: I'd love to, but we don't have the money.

Angie: You pay me time and a half for overtime. You could hire a full-time assistant for about that, and I could stop doing overtime. That way, you would also have someone to cover for me when I go on vacation or get sick.

Boss: Can you do the numbers for me?

Angie: Here, I already have.

Boss: You've sold me.

In this scenario, Angie has a relationship of mutual respect with her boss. She had allowed herself to slip into an unhealthy pattern of overworking because she had been eager for his approval and hoped for a raise or a bonus. Now, after considering her options, Angie brokered a change. When she talked to her boss, she was careful to frame the problem as a mutual one, and the solution as mutually advantageous.

EXERCISE: ADDRESS A LONG-STANDING PROBLEM WITH DIALOGUE

Choose a long-standing problem that you have decided to address by speaking up. Write out a dialogue on a separate piece of paper. Include setting up a time to talk. Express your perspective of the problem, your feelings, and what you want, along with how you would expect the other person to respond to you. If you anticipate resistance, remember to respond to the other person's attempts to derail you by acknowledging that you have heard his or her point, then returning to your own point. Remember, it's important to negotiate a win-win solution (see chapter 7).

Addressing an Immediate Problem

When possible, it is best to deal with boundary violations when they happen. The violation can be symptomatic of a long-standing problem. In this next scenario, Angie has tolerated her older sister Sylvia's superior attitude since she was a kid. Sylvia has a pattern of discounting what Angie says and justifying her own hurtful remarks. Angie decided to confront Sylvia when she made yet another dig about Angie's weight.

Angie: Sylvia, I notice that we haven't been together five minutes and you have already told me how fat I look, and how my clothes don't fit any more.

Sylvia: I'm just trying to help. I know you are unhappy about your weight and need some encouragement from those who care about you.

Angie: What you're saying to me really hurts my feelings and pisses me off. This is not news to me. I have heard this from you many times before. I think that it is not constructive feedback; it's a put-down under the guise of sisterly concern.

Sylvia: You're just being overly sensitive.

Angie: (ignoring the fact that Sylvia has just discounted her feelings so the conversation doesn't get sidetracked) Sylvia, tell me what I just said.

Sylvia: You said that I'm putting you down when I express my concern about your weight problem. Well I'm not . . .

Angie: Actually what I said is that when you tell me many times that I'm fat and my clothes don't fit, I feel angry and hurt. Perhaps you mean well, but your repetition of the same criticisms is not constructive. In fact, it feels destructive to me. Hearing these things from my sister really hurts.

Sylvia: So you're saying that my comments about your weight problem hurt your feelings. Is that right?

Angie: Right.

Sylvia: And they're not helpful?

Angie: Right.

Sylvia: I'm just trying to motivate you.

Angie: This isn't the way.

Sylvia: What can I do to help you lose weight and be happy again?

Angie: That's my responsibility to figure out, and I think I'm making some progress. I need you to just be my sister, not my keeper. I'd be really pleased if you didn't say anything about my weight problem for a while. Maybe you could say something nice about me occasionally.

Sylvia: I think I can do that. I'm sorry for being a nag. You will point it out if I slip?

Angie: Oh, yes.

Clearly Angie has a long way to go with her sister, but she has stood up for herself on this important issue. This time, it was enough to address the single issue of her sister putting her down about her weight. In a later discussion she can address how her sister discounts her feelings, justifies saying hurtful things under the cloak of sisterly concern, and many other problems. Little by little, by standing up for her perception of reality, her opinions, her feelings, and her wants, she will gradually develop a more egalitarian relationship with her big sister.

EXERCISE: STANDING UP FOR YOURSELF AT THE MOMENT OF VIOLATION

Think of a time recently when someone violated a boundary of yours, and you didn't let them know about it. Pretend to be back in that moment, and write out a dialogue in which you let them know they did it. Like in the example with Angie and Sylvia, begin with the boundary violation. Be sure to include the facts as you see them, your opinion, your feelings, and what you want. If you keep your message short and simple, the other person should be able to reflect back to you what he or she heard if you ask them to. If necessary, state your message in small pieces, or rephrase what you said. The next time a violation similar to this one occurs, you will be ready to protect yourself at the moment. Write out the entire dialogue on a separate piece of paper.

In this chapter you have considered those situations where you are operating from a one-down position in a relationship. As discussed, you can be in a one-down position because another person has legitimate power. You can also allow it to happen, by not standing up for what is important to you. After thinking about why you do this, you have come up with some healthy options to pursue.

CHAPTER 9

Dealing with Strong Emotions: Communicating with People in Pain

Miranda was devastated. At forty-eight, she had just been diagnosed with breast cancer. Her mother had died of the disease eleven years earlier. Her first call was to her husband, Raymond, who headed home from work the minute he heard. Miranda was just hanging up the phone when he arrived.

"I called both surgeons," she whispered into Raymond's shoulder, tears streaming down her cheeks. "I can't believe no one has an opening. The best guy couldn't see me until the middle of next week!" "It's going to be okay," Raymond reassured her as he moved out of the hug. "It's *not* going to be okay!" Miranda wailed. "I can't wait until next week to do something about it." "It must be okay to wait, or the doctors would have made time to see you," suggested Raymond. "That's crazy!" yelled Miranda. "The doctors couldn't care less. Mom died of this and I'm going to die too! And what's going to happen to the kids?" She broke into tears again. Raymond listened helplessly for a minute before offering some more reassurance: "People don't die from breast cancer as frequently anymore. Treatment's much better than it was when your mom got diagnosed." Miranda ran to her bedroom, where she threw herself on the bed, curled up into a fetal position, and lay racked with sobs. Raymond stood alone in the kitchen, feeling confused, bewildered, and completely at a loss.

Learning how to communicate effectively with people in pain can offer many rewards. The most significant is your ability to facilitate the healing of those you love who are in pain. Supporting someone through a painful experience can build a deeper, more meaningful relationship. You can also model skills that others can use when you are in pain and need the same support.

COMMON MISTAKES

Despite the best of intentions, Raymond was not able to give Miranda the support and help she desperately needed. However, responding appropriately to someone in pain is easier said than done. Too often your own discomfort with strong negative feelings gets in the way of being empathic. When your attempts fail, it's usually because you've fallen into one of the following common patterns.

- **Minimizing or Discounting Feelings.** "Calm down," "you're overreacting," "there, there," "don't worry," and "there's nothing to be afraid of," are all examples of attempts at reassurance that in fact minimize or discount the speaker's feelings. When you try to talk people out of their feelings, it only increases their feelings of isolation and pain.

- **Giving advice.** The words are barely out of the other person's mouth and you're offering helpful suggestions. Unsolicited advice carries the implicit message that not only is this person incapable of solving his or her own problem but that you're not really interested in how he or she is feeling. You just care about fixing the problem.

- **Interrogating.** Interrogating involves asking a barrage of questions in an effort to gather enough information to solve the problem. This response also implies that you're not really interested in the speaker's pain.

- **Blaming.** Blaming the victim for his or her pain is a way to disown any of your own responsibility for someone's feelings. The reasoning behind this response is if this person feels bad, he or she must have done something to deserve it.

- **Deflecting.** When someone begins to express pain, you make a joke or change the subject to something that's less painful. Rather than being a positive shift of focus, this response gives the other person the message that you can't (or don't want to) cope with the pain he or she feels.

- **Justifying or explaining.** Instead of listening to the feelings and trying to really understand the pain, you try to explain or to justify why the circumstances occurred that might have led to these feelings. Your rationale is that, with understanding, the pain will simply go away.

- **Sparring.** No matter what someone says, you're ready to debate, to disagree. As a result, the other person will never feel really heard; you're so quick with your verbal jabs, there's no time to listen.

EXERCISE: RECOGNIZING COMMON MISTAKES

Read the following dialogues. Then in the right-hand column identify the type of mistaken pattern demonstrated in that dialogue.

Dialogue	What was the mistake?
1. Isabelle: I made a complete fool of myself in class today. In the middle of my presentation, I went completely blank and forgot what I was going to say. I felt utterly humiliated. *Don:* I'm sure it wasn't so terrible. Probably no one will even remember it by next class.	
2. Paul: I've been sacked! I can't believe it! After thirteen years of loyalty, he just threw me out, without even a thank you! *Mischa:* Why would he have done that? Were you not producing enough? Were you spending too much time online?	
3. Tim: Bobbie gave me back my ring yesterday. I feel like my life is over. I don't *want* to live. *Patrick:* Hey! Jay just told me that if I got to work late one more time *my* life was over! Maybe we could jump from the bridge together and put everyone out of their misery!	
4. Karen: I wish I were dead! *Mom:* What happened? *Karen:* Everyone's been invited to Cathy's party except me. *Mom:* How do you know? Have you talked to Cathy? Is this because of the business with the sleepover?	
5. Chris: My boss went off at me today in front of the whole software department. I forgot to send the demo on time and it lost us the account. Oh God! What's going to happen now? *Yolande:* Well, your boss has been under a lot of stress lately, dealing with the buyout and everything. I'll bet if he weren't so stressed, he wouldn't have yelled in front of the group. That's not usually his style, is it?	
6. Evelyn: I'm so mad I could spit! How dare he call me names in front of the kids? *Wendy:* He didn't really call you names. *Evelyn:* He did too! He called me an emotional washrag. *Wendy:* That's not really calling names. *Evelyn:* Of course it is. And I can't stand it when you argue like this! *Wendy:* I'm not arguing; I'm just clarifying the point. And anyway, it wasn't really in front of the kids.	
7. Gary: Linda, I just found this vial in Jason's backpack when I was looking for the jacket I lent him. I think these pills are Ecstasy. And I hate to admit it, but I've had a sneaking suspicion that he's been smoking pot with his friends. *Linda:* Well, you'd better find him right now and confront him. And taking him to the chemical dependency clinic is probably the second step. I'd do it now before he has a chance to prepare his answers.	

Answers:

1. Minimizing or discounting feelings

2. Blaming

3. Deflecting

4. Interrogating

5. Justifying or explaining

6. Sparring

7. Giving advice

COMPASSIONATE LISTENING

The first step of a compassionate response is to listen to the other person and let this person know that you're listening, especially to his or her feelings. To really listen involves putting aside your discomfort and all your automatic, instinctive responses and letting people talk in whatever way they need to. Letting them know that you're listening involves acknowledging their pain by paraphrasing back to them what you've heard them say (focusing particularly on the feelings expressed).

If Raymond (in the initial example) had responded compassionately to Miranda's fear and grief, the interaction might have looked more like this:

Miranda: (whispering) I called both surgeons. I can't believe no one has an opening. The best guy couldn't see me until the middle of next week!

Raymond: (holding Miranda close) Honey, I'm so sorry, you must be feeling so scared.

Miranda: (wailing) I can't wait until next week to do something about it!

Raymond: (still holding her) I know. Next week must feel like forever right now.

Miranda: (whispering again) I'm going to die, and what's going to happen to the kids?

Raymond: You love those kids so much! Well, I'm here honey, and together we're going to fight this and we're going to get through this.

Miranda: (whispering) I'm so scared.

Raymond: What can I do?

Miranda: Keep holding me.

In this scenario, Miranda still had her feelings of fear and grief, but instead of feeling isolated in her pain, she felt supported and loved. When held with such compassion, Miranda could more easily move toward a gradual healing of her feelings, and eventually toward assessing her alternatives and choosing appropriate action. Her feelings will no doubt surface again during her struggles with cancer, but her relationship with Raymond will only deepen with the interactions.

OTHER COMPASSIONATE RESPONSES

Once the person in pain knows that you're listening, you can choose from several specific categories of response to accompany the compassionate active listening described above.

- **Offering support:** "How can I help you through this?" People in pain often know what kind of support they need, but it may be hard for them to ask for it. Offering it removes this barrier.

- **Asking for elaboration:** You can say, "Tell me more about it," or "Then what happened?" You may not be able to understand what the person's pain is about from their initial expressions. It's okay to ask for elaboration when the question comes from a genuine desire to be empathic. Moreover, sometimes people in pain need to tell their story, and this telling itself can alleviate some of the pain.

- **Exploring fears or worst-case scenarios:** "What are your fears?" or "What's the worst thing that could come from this?" are questions you could ask. Sometimes clarifying the worst possible outcome can enable someone to focus on a more realistic possibility and alleviate some pain.

- **Reducing isolation:** It helps to say, "Together we can get through this." Often feelings of isolation accompany intense emotional pain. Reducing that sense of isolation can facilitate the path to healing.

- **Encouraging problem solving:** Ask, "What might you do about it?" People often feel totally overwhelmed by their pain. At the same time, they can experience any unsolicited advice you might give as intrusive and infantilizing. Encouraging problem solving stimulates their own abilities to determine what they need to do and usually is experienced as empowering.

- **Eliciting additional support:** It may help to say, "Is there anyone else you could talk to about this?" or "Who else could help you with this?" There's a direct relationship between social and emotional support and improved physical and emotional health. Helping people think about who else in their lives might be able to offer support can also serve to reduce isolation.

- **Stimulating coping resources:** Ask the person, "Has anything like this ever happened before?" or "How have you coped with this in the past?" Remembering a previous success can stimulate optimism and remind people of their coping strategies.

- **Understanding cognitive factors:** It may help to ask, "What are your thoughts about it?" or "What are you telling yourself about this?" Negative or self-critical cognitive statements can increase the intensity of someone's pain. Helping people understand what they're thinking can sometimes alleviate some of their pain.

■   **Expanding resources:** You can ask, "What organizations or agencies might be able to offer information or support around this?" Gathering information can be empowering in many circumstances. Helping the person determine where to go to gather that information or support can jump-start the process.

EXERCISE: WORKING ON COMPASSIONATE RESPONSES

Below are the first halves of each dialogue from the previous exercise. For the second half of each dialogue, write at least one compassionate listening response and an additional helpful response from the above list of possibilities. Remember that your goal is not to take away the pain, but rather to help these people feel supported so that they can do what they need to do to take care of themselves.

1. *Isabelle:*   I made a complete fool of myself in a staff meeting today. In the middle of my presentation, I went completely blank and forgot what I was going to say. I felt utterly humiliated.

   Don: _____

   _____

   _____

2. *Paul:*   I've been sacked! I can't believe it! After thirteen years of loyalty, he just threw me out, without even a thank you!

   Mischa: _____

   _____

   _____

3. *Tim:*   Bobbie gave me back my ring yesterday. I feel like my life is over. I don't *want* to live.

   Patrick: _____

   _____

   _____

4. *Karen:*   I wish I were dead! Everyone's been invited to Cathy's party except me.

   Mom: _____

   _____

   _____

5. *Chris:*   My boss went off at me today in front of the whole software department. I forgot to send the demo on time and it lost us the account. Oh God! What's going to happen now?

Yolande: _____

_____

_____

6. *Evelyn:*   I'm so mad I could spit! How dare he call me names in front of the kids?

Wendy: _____

_____

_____

7. *Gary:*   Linda, I just found this vial in Jason's backpack when I was looking for the jacket I lent him. I think these pills are Ecstasy. And I hate to admit it, but I've had a sneaking suspicion that he's been smoking pot with his friends.

Linda: _____

_____

_____

Possible answers:

1. *Don:* (compassionate listening) It must have been awful to have everyone watching and waiting for you to continue speaking. (understanding cognitive factors) What are your thoughts about it? (offering support) Is there anything I can do to help you feel better?

2. *Mischa:* (compassionate listening) You've put in so much of your time and effort for this job and you must feel totally unappreciated. (encouraging problem solving) What do you think you might do about it? (expanding resources) Do you think talking to the union would be helpful?

3. *Patrick:* (compassionate listening) You must be so hurt. (offering support) How can I help? (asking for elaboration) What happened?

4. *Mom:* (compassionate listening) Oh honey, I'm sorry. That's disappointing! (asking for elaboration and reducing isolation) Tell me about it. (offering support) How can I help right now?

5. *Yolande:* (compassionate listening) You sound scared about what the boss might do. (exploring fears or worst-case scenarios) What's your worst fear? (reducing isolation) Well, whatever happens, we're in this together and we'll be okay.

6. *Wendy:* (compassionate listening) It must be infuriating for you! (encouraging problem solving) What can you do about it? (stimulating coping resources) Has he done this in the past? How have you coped with it?

7. *Linda:* (compassionate listening) Oh no! Our worst fears! (expanding resources and encouraging problem solving) Do you think we should consult with one of the teen chemical dependency clinics about how to handle it? (reducing isolation) Well, at least we can do this together.

PUTTING IT ALL TOGETHER

Each of the different categories of response can be used when responding to people in pain, depending on their level of pain. Compassionate listening (acknowledging and paraphrasing the feelings) is the most appropriate strategy in the beginning when someone's pain is most intense. Feeling heard will alleviate some pain, at which point asking for elaboration, offering support, and reducing isolation are useful strategies. Exploring worst-case scenarios, encouraging problem solving, eliciting additional support, stimulating coping resources, understanding cognitive factors, and expanding resources are all more elaborate responses.

EXERCISE: PRACTICING YOUR RESPONSE

Read the following interaction and write responses based on what you've learned about compassionate listening in the spaces provided. Possible second categories of response are listed in parentheses as clues.

    Raelene has answered her front doorbell to find her best friend standing on the stoop, disheveled and distraught.

Raelene: Anne, what's happened? Come in!

Anne: A man jumped me in the parking lot at work. I didn't know where else to go. I couldn't go home.

Raelene: (compassionate listening, reducing isolation) _____

_____

Anne: I don't know what to do!

Raelene: (taking Anne's hand and asking for elaboration) _____

_____

Anne: I was working late on the Barron case. Nobody else was in the building, which is a little
    unusual, but not terribly. I noticed that the lights in the parking lot were out, so I started
    walking towards my car. I thought I heard someone laugh softly and then I heard footsteps
    and I started running, but he . . . he grabbed my arm and threw me down. He must have been
    hiding somewhere. I don't know. He was cursing and muttering obscenities at me and trying
    to rip my coat. I kicked and hit and screamed as loudly as I could, even though I knew there
    wasn't anyone around to hear. But I guess he didn't know that and he got up and ran away.

Raelene: (compassionate listening, exploring fears or worst-case scenarios) _____

_____

Anne: I know it's silly, but I'm afraid he might know where I live and be waiting there for me!

Raelene: (offering support, reducing isolation) _____

_____

Anne: Thanks Rae, you're such a good friend.

Raelene: (encouraging problem solving) _____

_____

Anne: No. I suppose I should, though.

Raelene: (understanding cognitive factors) _____

_____

Anne: Well, it's probably crazy, but I keep thinking that they're going to think I'm just some hysterical woman and that they won't really try to catch him.

Raelene: (understanding cognitive factors) _____

_____

Anne: And then he'd find out and get even madder and come and find me and kill me.

Raelene: (compassionate listening) _____

_____

Anne: Yeah, crazy, huh? I'd better call them.

Raelene: (reducing isolation, offering support) _____

_____

Anne: Thanks. I would like that. Would you make the call for me? I'm not thinking straight. I guess that's obvious. I'm sure there are other things I should be doing, but I just keep seeing his face and remembering how frightened I was, and I can't think of anything else.

Raelene: (stimulating coping resources, reducing isolation) _____

_____

Anne: Yes, you're right. I know we can. Okay, let's call.

Possible response:

The following is a sample of possible responses that Raelene could have made in the face of Anne's pain:

Raelene: Anne, what's happened? Come in!

Anne: A man jumped me in the parking lot at work. I didn't know where else to go. I can't go home.

Raelene: (compassionate listening, reducing isolation) I'm so sorry, what a nightmare! And of course you came here, that's what friends are for.

Anne: I don't know what to do!

Raelene: (taking Anne's hand and asking for elaboration) Tell me about what happened.

Anne: I was working late on the Barron case. Nobody else was in the building, which is a little unusual, but not terribly. I noticed that the lights in the parking lot were out, so I started walking towards my car. I thought I heard someone laugh softly and then I heard footsteps and I started running, but he . . . he grabbed my arm and threw me down. He must have been hiding somewhere. I don't know. He was cursing and muttering obscenities at me and trying to rip my coat. I kicked and hit and screamed as loudly as I could, even though I knew there wasn't anyone around to hear. But I guess he didn't know that and he got up and ran away.

Raelene: (compassionate listening, exploring fears or worst-case scenarios) It sounds terrifying! (pause) What are your fears right now?

Anne: I know it's silly but I'm afraid he might know where I live and be waiting there for me!

Raelene: (offering support, reducing isolation) You can stay here with me as long as you like.

Anne: Thanks Rae, you're such a good friend.

Raelene: (encouraging problem solving) No problem. Have you thought about what you might do about it, though? Call the police or anyone?

Anne: No. I suppose I should, though.

Raelene: (understanding cognitive factors) What are your thoughts about it?

Anne: Well, it's probably crazy, but I keep thinking that they're going to think I'm just some hysterical woman and that they won't really try to catch him.

Raelene: (understanding cognitive factors) And then?

Anne: And then he'd find out and get even madder and come and find me and kill me.

Raelene: (compassionate listening) No wonder you're not so eager to call the police!

Anne: Yeah, crazy, huh? I'd better call them.

Raelene: (reducing isolation, offering support) I can call, or we could just go down to the station if you want. You don't have to go through any more of this on your own.

Anne: Thanks. I would like that. Would you make the call for me? I'm not thinking straight. I guess that's obvious. I'm sure there are other things I should be doing, but I just keep seeing his face and remembering how frightened I was, and I can't think of anything else.

Raelene: (stimulating coping resources, reducing isolation) Well, we'll work it out together. Remember when mom died and you helped me through that? I never thought I'd feel okay again, but I did. We can do this!

Anne: Yes, you're right. I know we can. Okay, let's call.

WHEN YOU'RE THE SOURCE OF THE PAIN

When someone is angry at you, feels shamed by or afraid of you, you're likely to be at the receiving end of criticism and blame. It's harder to listen compassionately and respond helpfully at those times. Your instinct probably is to get defensive, to fire up your own anger and respond in kind. However, if your goal is to help the person in pain, then your focus has to be on what he or she needs rather than on your own reactions and impulses.

Sometimes criticism can be accurate and constructive, and the best strategy is to acknowledge it. But in order to determine the validity of the complaint, you must first understand it. Use the strategy of *asking for elaboration* ("Can you give me examples of what you're referring to?") until you're clear about the nature of the problem and its validity. If valid, *acknowledging* it nondefensively (without sarcasm or justifications) can defuse the situation. When appropriate, an *apology* goes a long way.

Ricky: You're going with Todd to the Christmas party! I told you I liked him! I can't believe you're doing this. You've ruined my life!

Ed: (compassionate listening and apology) Yes, I am going with him. I'm sorry it's so painful for you.

It can be helpful to use the additional strategy of *offering support*, though you may not be willing or able to comply with what is requested.

Ed: Is there anything I can do to help with your pain?

Ricky: Tell Todd you've changed your mind and can't go with him to the party.

Ed: I'm sorry. I'm unwilling to do that.

How to Use Clouding

If criticism is not valid, you need to switch to the assertive strategy of *clouding* as an accompaniment to compassionate listening. (See chapter 5.) Clouding involves honestly and carefully looking for the grain of truth in the criticism while maintaining your own perspective on the situation. Again, there are three ways of clouding. Take the statement, "You never make love to me anymore. You're sick of me and this relationship is dying."

1. *Agreeing in part* involves acknowledging the part of the criticism you can agree with and ignoring the rest: "You're right, it has been a while since we made love."

2. *Agreeing in probability* acknowledges that there might be a chance (albeit tiny) that the criticism is valid: "It's possible that I haven't initiated lovemaking enough lately."

3. *Agreeing in principle* involves acknowledging that if the condition described exists, then the conclusion drawn is likely (without either confirming or denying whether the condition actually exists). "It's true that if frequent lovemaking is a sign of a healthy relationship, then our relationship is in trouble."

Any of these three kinds of responses could follow a compassionate statement that acknowledges the person's pain: "Sounds like you're feeling unappreciated in the relationship right now."

EXERCISE: PRACTICING CLOUDING

Respond to the criticism below with each of the three types of clouding.

"You stole that account from me! That was my account! Vesser all but said he was going to give it to me, and suddenly he gave it to you."

Agreeing in part: _____

_____

Agreeing in probability: _____

_____

Agreeing in principle: _____

_____

Possible answers:

Agreeing in part: "You're right, Vesser did give it to me rather suddenly."

Agreeing in probability: "You may be right that Vesser had planned to give it to you."

Agreeing in principle: "I can imagine that if Vesser had suggested that he was planning to give you the account, then it would feel like yours."

In conclusion, when people you care about are in pain, it's not enough to rely on your instincts on how to respond. It's important to know what kinds of responses are likely to make them feel shut down or more isolated, and to respond in ways that will help them feel supported and encouraged to take care of themselves in the manner that is best for them.

PART 3

Out in the World: Friends, Family, and Work

CHAPTER 10

Sensitizing Yourself to Gender: Understanding the Opposite Sex

Since beginning her relationship with Len a year ago, and more seriously since moving into his beautiful suburban house, Rosemary had been having trouble with poison oak. She wasn't touching it herself; she'd made that mistake once with disastrous results and had become extremely conscientious about avoiding it at all costs. But Len, who seemed immune to poison oak, had the long-standing habit of wandering around his couple acres, pulling up stray shoots of the weed in a bid to rid his property of it. It was a habit based in the best of intentions, yet despite these good intentions, Rosemary kept breaking out in nasty, itchy rashes two or three days after each of Len's excursions. Len tried many things to ensure Rosemary's safety, from wearing gardening gloves to stripping off all his clothes in the laundry room, putting them straight in the washing machine, and scrubbing himself down in the shower with special soap. Nothing seemed to work. Finally after her tenth outbreak, Rosemary had had enough. "You just can't pull it up anymore!" she stormed. "You can't tell me how to spend my free time!" Len countered indignantly. "It's meditative and I want to try some other remedies first." Rosemary was horrified, and her tone verged on hysterical. "I've gotten poison oak ten times now; I can't believe you're not concerned enough about me to *want* to stop pulling it up!" Len was rigid in his resistance. "We haven't tried everything yet. And I'm not willing for you to tell me how to spend my free time," he repeated.

Len and Rosemary's problem was typical of a lot of couples who find it difficult to bridge the gender gap. Understanding how your partner sees and reacts to the world differently from you can enable you to communicate more effectively. Doing so increases the chances that your needs and goals—and your partner's needs and goals—will be met. This, in turn, provides the foundation of a more supportive relationship with increased intimacy.

GENDER DIFFERENCES

In *You Just Don't Understand*, by Deborah Tannen (1990), the key differences in communication styles between men and women are explained as reflecting the different orientation men and women have to relationships in general. Women, according to Tannen, see the world through a lens of intimacy and connection and use communication not simply as a means of exchanging information but also to create intimacy. Men, however, see the world through the lens of status and independence, and much of their communication reflects patterns of challenges and parrying of challenges. Needless to say, this can lead to painful misunderstandings, made especially painful because they occur so often with the person to whom you look for the most support and understanding: your spouse or partner.

Len and Rosemary's struggle is an example of gender differences leading to painful misunderstanding. Rosemary is focusing on her desire to feel supported and at one with Len. Through her lens of connection and emotional intimacy, it's hard for her to understand why Len doesn't *want* to stop pulling up the poison oak. Len, on the other hand, cherishes his independence, and is appalled at what he interprets as an attempt by Rosemary to order him to stop behaving in ways that he enjoys. If he agrees to stop pulling up poison oak, he is accepting that their relationship is one in which Rosemary has the power to tell him what to do, thereby limiting his freedom. His refusal to stop is interpreted by Rosemary as defining their relationship as one in which he doesn't care about his actions' impact on her health.

Men are from Mars, Women Are from Venus (Gray 1992) suggests that men and women are so different in their communication styles that they might as well have come from different planets. Gray also suggests that men talk primarily to gather or exchange information, while women talk for a host of other additional reasons, including exploring their thoughts and feelings, feeling better when they're upset, and creating intimacy. Gray believes that when men are stressed, their tendency is to retreat from others (including their partners) in order to internally process and solve problems. Under these same circumstances, women want to connect (especially with their partners)—to process and feel better by talking. These opposing tendencies often lead men to feel nagged and harassed when their partners push them to "talk about what's going on," and then to feel blamed and criticized when they won't. These same tendencies often leave women feeling abandoned and unloved when their partners retreat, and invalidated and misunderstood when they seem unwilling to "just listen."

These differences, innate or learned, can be seen clearly from early childhood. Whether we like it or not, they exist, and the better we are able to negotiate the resulting minefields, the better our relationships will be. This chapter will help you understand the ways in which men and women's communication styles differ, and will teach you some new ways to express yourself that will help decrease the number of painful misunderstandings in your relationships with members of the opposite sex.

EXERCISE: IDENTIFYING GENDER DIFFERENCES

Look at the following twenty-six communication traits, and for each one decide whether it best describes a man or a woman. This list was adapted from McKay, Davis, and Fanning (1995).

This communication trait best describes a	Man	Woman
1. Makes decisions using coercion, persuasion, or majority rule	_____	_____
2. Doesn't ask for help, advice, or directions	_____	_____
3. Speaks up more in public	_____	_____
4. Yearns for intimacy	_____	_____
5. Is motivated by independence and autonomy	_____	_____
6. Is quick to empathize and sympathize	_____	_____
7. Wants to understand others' problems	_____	_____
8. Wants approval of peers	_____	_____
9. Sticks to business	_____	_____
10. Decides by consensus	_____	_____
11. Tends to relate as rivals	_____	_____
12. Prefers interdependence and cooperation	_____	_____
13. Seeks status	_____	_____
14. Wants respect of peers	_____	_____
15. Wants to share problems	_____	_____
16. Wants to solve problems	_____	_____
17. Asks for help, advice, and directions	_____	_____
18. Attends to the details of feelings	_____	_____
19. Seeks connection	_____	_____
20. Keeps problems to themselves	_____	_____
21. Mixes personal and business talk	_____	_____
22. Attends to the details of fact	_____	_____
23. Tends to relate as equals	_____	_____
24. Speaks up more in private	_____	_____
25. Is quick to give advice and analysis	_____	_____
26. Yearns for space	_____	_____

Answers: Traits more characteristic of a man: numbers 1, 2, 3, 5, 9, 11, 13, 14, 16, 20, 22, 25, 26. Traits more characteristic of a woman: numbers 4, 6, 7, 8, 10, 12, 15, 17, 18, 19, 21, 23, 24.

Some of these traits may be shown by both men and women, yet each trait is generally more characteristic of one gender. Neither group of communication traits is better or worse. What's important is that you understand the differences.

One of the most difficult realities you have to face is that when you relate to the other gender the way you would like him or her to relate to you, he or she doesn't feel gratified. In fact, the result is usually quite the opposite. The other person feels invalidated or ignored, criticized or unfairly blamed, or burdened by what was supposed to be a thoughtful response. Because men and women approach the world through different lenses and have different needs, it's essential to learn how to communicate in ways that can best be heard. For each of the situations described below you will find points to remember, and communication rules written separately for men and women.

HOW TO EXPRESS NEGATIVE FEELINGS

It's always hard to tell someone you love that you're upset with something they've done or said. It's easy for both men and women to feel blamed or criticized. What follows are the reminders and rules of communication for women and then for men.

If You Are a Woman Expressing Negative Feelings

There are three points to remember:

1. He feels easily blamed and criticized.

2. He needs to feel appreciated, accepted, and trusted.

3. It's not your job to try and improve him.

The Rules for Women Expressing

1. Start with a positive, appreciative statement ("I know how hard you work . . .").

2. Keep it short and simple ("I didn't like it when you . . .").

3. Be factual without superlatives or generalizations (avoid "You always . . .").

4. Specify what you would like ("I would like it if you would . . .").

The Rules for Men Receiving

A. Don't respond defensively (remind yourself that she's telling you something about *herself* and *her* feelings).

B. Look at her when she's speaking to you.

C. Let her know that you've heard her ("Okay, I hear you . . .").

D. Let her know what you're willing to do ("I'd be willing to try . . .").

EXERCISE 1: EXPRESSING NEGATIVE FEELINGS OR MAKING A COMPLAINT

Read the following interaction between Robin and Bruce.

Robin: If you're going to do nothing but sit in front of the computer again tonight, I'm going to bed.

Bruce: Goodnight.

Robin: I can't believe you'd prefer to play that damned game than hang out with me.

Bruce: Why would I want to hang out with someone who does nothing but complain?

Robin: Well, if you ever showed me the least consideration, there'd be nothing to complain about.

In the space below, rewrite the interaction using the rules outlined above.

Robin: _____

_____

Bruce: _____

_____

Robin: _____

_____

Bruce: _____

_____

Robin: _____

_____

Possible rewrite:

Robin: (rule 1)I know you love zoning out on the computer after a hard day's work, and you deserve it. (rule 2) But I didn't like it when you were down here the whole evening yesterday. (rule 3) I felt unimportant, like you preferred to play alone than with me.

Bruce: (rules A and B) I just needed some time to relax. But I guess I got carried away; I can understand you feeling left out.

Robin: Thank you. (rule 4) What I'd really like is if you would set aside some time for us to hang out together in the evenings. Maybe we could play a little ourselves.

Bruce: Mmm. Could be fun! (rule D) I'd be willing to turn the game off after an hour or so. Is that tolerable?

Robin: That would be great! I'll be upstairs when you're done.

If You Are a Man Expressing Negative Feelings

Here are three points to remember:

1. She knows you're upset even (or especially) if you don't say anything.

2. She feels easily unloved by your silence and withdrawal.

3. A physical gesture of affection goes a long way.

The Rules for Men Expressing

1. If you need time alone to think, tell her you'll be back ("I want to talk with you, but right now I need . . .").

2. Start with a statement of reassurance ("I love you . . .").

3. Keep it short and simple ("I didn't like it when you . . .").

4. Be factual without superlatives or generalizations (avoid "You always . . .").

5. Specify what you would like ("I would like it if you would . . .").

The Rules for Women Receiving

A. Don't pursue him if you know he's upset and says he needs time to think before talking.

B. Express appreciation when he's ready to talk.

C. Let him know that you've heard ("Okay, I hear you . . .").

D. Let him know what you're willing to do ("I'd be willing to try . . .").

EXERCISE 2: EXPRESSING NEGATIVE FEELINGS OR MAKING A COMPLAINT

Read the following interaction between Ashley and Peter.

Peter: What the hell did you think you were doing, criticizing me in front of my parents?

Ashley: I wasn't criticizing you; I just pointed out a more efficient way to fix the shelf.

Peter: Well, if I'd needed your help, I'd have asked for it. If not, stay out of my business.

Ashley: Well, aren't you Mr. Cheerful tonight.

In the space below, rewrite the interaction using the rules outlined above.

Peter: _____

_____

Ashley: _____

_____

Peter: _____

_____

Ashley: _____

_____

Possible rewrite:

Peter: (rules 2, 3, and 4) Honey, I hated it when you criticized me in front of my parents tonight. It felt like you didn't think I was capable of fixing the shelf on my own.

Ashley: (rule C) I didn't mean to criticize you. I didn't realize it would sound that way. But I get it that it did.

Peter: (rule 5) Unless I ask for your help, I'd really like you to trust that I'm competent enough to get the job done.

Ashley: (rule D) I do trust you sweetheart, and I'm going to try my hardest not to offer unsolicited advice like that. I really get how patronizing that must sound.

HOW TO ASK FOR HELP OR SUPPORT

For different reasons, it's hard for both men and women to ask their partners for support. Feeling competent is important for men, and having to ask for help triggers feelings of incompetence. Instead, they withdraw and attempt to solve their problems alone. Only if this strategy fails will they ask (usually a buddy), and then men expect to get only the information requested. Since men can experience unsolicited offers of help as expressions of lack of trust in their competence, men don't usually offer unsolicited help to their partners. Women, on the other hand, are often happy to anticipate their partners' needs and attempt to fulfill those needs without being asked. Expecting the same behavior from their partners, however, they resist asking for help until they feel so burdened or overwhelmed that their eventual request becomes a criticism. It is particularly important, therefore, for women to be able—and willing—to ask for help before this shift occurs from request to criticism.

If You Are a Woman Asking for Help

Here are three points to remember:

1. Men easily hear requests as demands.

2. He needs to feel able to say no, and have it be acceptable.

3. He needs to feel appreciated for the things he does.

The Rules for Women Asking

1. Practice asking for something that your partner already does.

2. Ask clearly and briefly (no reasons or justifications).

3. Use "would you" and "will you" rather than "could you" and "can you." ('Could' and "can" question a person's *ability* to do something; men can feel manipulated when a request is implied in a question about their ability to do something.)

4. Express appreciation when he says yes.

5. Practice asking (using "would you" and "will you") for something bigger, and accept it graciously if he says no (don't argue, criticize, or express disappointment; simply remain silent—sometimes in the face of silence, a no becomes a yes).

6. Express appreciation when he says yes.

EXERCISE 1: ASKING FOR HELP OR SUPPORT

Read the following interaction between Carol and Jeff.

Carol: I've been running the kids around all day and trying to clean up in between; the least you could do is take out the trash when you see it overflowing!

Jeff: (silence)

Carol: Well, *could* you take it out before I have to wash the kitchen floor again?

Jeff: Maybe.

Carol: Maybe? What kind of an answer is that?

Jeff: Maybe I could take it out before you have to wash the kitchen floor again.

Carol: Why don't you just say you're not going to help?

Jeff: I don't like being ordered around.

In the space below, rewrite the interaction using the rules outlined above.

Carol: _____

_____

Jeff: _____

_____

Carol: _____

_____

Jeff: _____

_____

Possible rewrite:

Carol: (rules 1, 2, and 3) Jeff honey, would you please take out the garbage?

Jeff: In a bit.

Carol: (rule 4) Thanks sweetie. I really appreciate your help.

Jeff: No problem.

If You Are a Man Asking for Help

Here are three points to remember:

1. Women are likely to say yes, even if they're feeling burdened.

2. She needs to feel cherished and loved.

3. If she says no, she's really overwhelmed.

The Rules for Men Asking

1. Ask clearly and briefly.

2. Offer an exchange (i.e., "Would you please _____ , and is there something I could do for you in return?").

3. Express gratitude and love.

EXERCISE 2: ASKING FOR HELP OR SUPPORT

Read the following interaction between Nadia and Ahmed.

Ahmed: Where's my yellow striped shirt?

Nadia: I don't know. Maybe it's still at the dry cleaners.

Ahmed: Could you pick it up on your way home from work?

Nadia: I already have to pick up the kids, supervise their homework, and start dinner.

Ahmed: Well, it's not as if it would take very long to pick up one shirt.

Nadia: No, so why couldn't you just do it?

Ahmed: Forget it.

In the space below, rewrite the interaction using the rules outlined above.

Ahmed: _____

_____

Nadia: _____

_____

Ahmed: _____

_____

Nadia _____

_____

Ahmed: _____

_____

Nadia: _____

_____

Ahmed: _____

_____

Possible rewrite:

Ahmed: Nadia, do you know where my yellow striped shirt is?

Nadia: Could it still be at the dry cleaners?

Ahmed: Probably. (rule 1) Would you mind picking it up for me tomorrow?

Nadia: I have to pick up the kids, supervise their homework, and start dinner.

Ahmed: (rule 2) Would it make it easier if I picked up some takeout on the way home?

Nadia: That would be great! Then, of course, I'll pick up your shirt.

Ahmed: (rule 3) Thanks, babe. Then I can wear it to my meeting on Friday.

COMMUNICATING SUPPORT

When men are stressed, they're likely to want to take some time out and avoid the problem by zoning out in front of the television or computer or by reading the paper. When they're ready to try to solve the problem, they're likely to want to do it alone. Talking is not perceived as being of particular value in a stressful situation. For women, on the other hand, talking is the single-most important tool in reducing stress and regaining a sense of equilibrium. It's through talking that women explore their thoughts and feelings and feel better about their situation. For both sexes, therefore, communicating support to your partner often involves behaving in ways that feel completely counterintuitive.

If You Are a Woman Communicating Support

Here are three points to remember:

1. If he's made a mistake or failed in some way, he knows it.

2. He needs to feel competent, by being trusted, appreciated, and accepted.

3. He needs to feel okay about not talking about his stress.

The Rules for Women Communicating

1. Let your partner know briefly and clearly that you're available to talk about what's bothering him if he would like to.

2. Don't harass him if he says no.

3. Don't point out ways in which he could improve or do things better next time; don't say "I told you so." Don't give advice or offer suggestions.

4. Express trust in his ability to solve his problem.

The Rules for Men Receiving

A. If you need time alone or to zone out, remind your partner that it's time limited and that you'll be back.

B. If you've made a mistake, apologize to her.

EXERCISE 1: WORKING ON COMMUNICATING SUPPORT

Read the following interaction between Tina and Devon.

Tina: You seem upset about something. What's going on? Is this about getting us lost?

Devon: It's nothing.

Tina: It can't be nothing. You've got your sourpuss face on again.

Devon: I said it's nothing. Stop bugging me.

Tina: Okay, okay, but if you'd just talk about it, maybe you'd actually feel better and then I wouldn't have to walk on eggshells all day. Getting us lost isn't such a big deal. Of course, if you'd listened to my directions, maybe we wouldn't have gotten lost.

Devon: Maybe you could just leave me the hell alone. Then I'd actually feel better.

In the space below, rewrite the interaction using the rules outlined above.

Tina: _____

_____

Devon: _____

_____

Tina: _____

_____

Devon: _____

_____

Possible rewrite:

Tina: (rule 1) You seem upset about something. Want to talk about it?

Devon: (rule A) No thanks. Maybe later.

Tina: (rules 2, 3, and 4) I know you'll work it out. Let me know if I can help.

Devon: Thanks.

If You Are a Man Communicating Support

Here are three points to remember:

1. She needs to talk to feel better; if you let her talk, she will automatically feel better.

2. She needs to feel understood.

3. Your job is not to solve or fix anything.

The Rules for Men Communicating

1. Listen with 100 percent of your attention.

2. Look at her when she's talking.

3. Offer listening signals: "mmm," "yes," "I see," "uh huh," "wow." These don't necessarily imply agreement with what's being expressed.

4. Give physical signs of affection (take her hand, give her a hug).

5. Don't offer solutions, try and fix her negative feelings, or explain why she shouldn't feel the way she does.

6. Don't get defensive; remind yourself that she's just releasing steam.

The Rules for Women Receiving

A. Remind your partner that your feelings are yours and that he is not to blame for everything that feels bad in your life right now.

B. Express appreciation for him listening.

EXERCISE 2: WORKING ON COMMUNICATING SUPPORT

Read the following interaction between Rachael and Gideon.

Rachael: God, I'm so tired; I feel like I've been running around nonstop all day, without a moment to relax.

Gideon: So relax. No one asked you to run around all day.

Rachael: No one asked me to, but if I didn't do it, nothing would get done.

Gideon: Oh right! So it's my fault that you have to run around all day. If I did more, you wouldn't have to do so much. Is that what you're saying?

Rachael: No! It's just that with the new hours at work, I don't get as much time as I would like.

Gideon: So, tell your boss you want your old hours back.

Rachael: You just don't understand!

In the space below, rewrite the interaction using the rules outlined above:

Rachael: _____

_____

Gideon: _____

_____

Rachael: _____

_____

Gideon: _____

_____

Rachael: _____

_____

Gideon: _____

_____

Rachael: _____

_____

Possible rewrite:

Rachael: God, I'm so tired; I feel like I've been running around nonstop all day, without a moment to relax.

Gideon: (rules 3, 5, and 6) Wow!

Rachael: There's so much to do!

Gideon: (rules 3, 5, and 6) Mmm.

Rachael: And with my new hours at work, I don't get as much time as I would like.

Gideon: (rule 4) That's too bad. Come here, let me give you a hug.

Rachael: (rule B) Okay. I'm sure glad I have you to listen to me! Thanks.

EXERCISE: TAKING CHARGE OF YOUR OWN RELATIONSHIP

Think about your own special opposite-gender relationship, if you are in one. Pick the skill you'd like to focus on (expressing negative feelings or making a complaint, asking for help or support, or offering support). Then determine which specific area you'd like to address (what negative feelings you want to express, what you want to ask for support with, or what you want to offer support for). Write this information below:

The skill you'd like to focus on: _____

The specific area you want to address: _____

_____

What you would say to your partner (using the rules you've learned in this chapter): _____

_____

_____

_____

_____

By practicing the skills you've learned in this chapter, you will hopefully soon be on the path to a better, more supportive, and more intimate relationship with your partner. Or, if currently single, you'll be in a better position to communicate well in your next relationship.

CHAPTER 11

Making Contact: Meeting New People and Cultivating Friendships

Some of the benefits of learning to make contact are

- overcoming your fears about meeting new people

- having interesting conversations with new people

- gaining a richer life with more friends

While some people reading this chapter may simply need to fine-tune their social skills, many people are reluctant to introduce themselves to a new person because they are afraid of being rejected. If you are in this second group of people, you are like Jim who was always puzzled by how his friend Sam managed to have so many great women friends.

FACING YOUR FEARS

One day, Jim was visiting Sam in the city. As usual, he was curious about the key to Sam's active social life. As the two men were walking around, Jim discovered Sam's secret. Every time Sam saw an attractive woman, he made eye contact with her, smiled, and said "Hello, what do you think of this beautiful weather we're having?" or "Hello, I don't mean to be forward, but that's a nice-looking dress you're wearing. Where did you get it?" On the spot, he thought up a variety of mundane opening lines to get women's attention. At the end of the day, Jim asked Sam, "When you get rejected, doesn't it bother you? I couldn't stand being shot down like that. I'd feel like a complete fool."

Sam explained to Jim, "It's not the ones that got away that matter. It's the three nice women I met today who make it all worthwhile. The ones who didn't stop to talk all had their reasons. Where is it written that I should take their lack of interest personally? When I see a woman I want to get to know, I don't ask myself, "What is she going to think of me? What if she rejects me? That kind of thinking would stop me dead in my tracks. Everybody has different tastes, so it seems natural to me that not every woman I like will feel the same about me. If a woman I want to get to know better isn't interested in me; it's unfortunate, but it's not the end of the world. I can feel good about myself for trying to get what I want. I don't have to hit a home run every time I'm at bat."

Jim realized that he and Sam perceived reality very differently in this area. Indeed, cognitive behavioral therapists would say that this was the key to Jim's social anxiety. It is not the event that causes your feelings; it is how you interpret the event that determines whether you feel confident, or anxious or some other emotion. Sam looks at an encounter with a new woman as an opportunity to enrich his life and he gets excited. Jim views a first encounter with a woman as an opportunity to be rejected, and he becomes anxious. Each man's beliefs can lead to a self-fulfilling prophecy. How can people like Jim change their thinking so that it is more like Sam's? Cognitive therapists recommend identifying your anxiety-provoking thoughts and then replacing them with thoughts that are rational, based in fact, and helpful. A good book on this topic is *The Shyness and Social Anxiety Workbook* (Antony and Swinson 2000).

Here are a few examples of how Jim might identify and challenge a few of his anxiety-provoking thoughts that inhibit him when he is with attractive women.

Anxious thought: "I won't have anything interesting to say."

Rational thought: "I can't predict the future, but I can plan to have some interesting things to talk about and I can ask questions. Even in movies, conversations aren't always interesting. In real life, a lot of what passes for conversation is downright boring. Conversation with a new person doesn't have to be interesting, as long as we get a chance to find out if we have anything in common."

Anxious thought: "She's going to think I'm a fool and tell me to get lost."

Rational thought: "I'm not a fortune teller, and not a mind reader, either. If she does tell me to take a hike, that just means we're not a good fit and I should be grateful I didn't waste any more time talking to her."

Anxious thought: "If she rejects me, that will prove I'm a loser."

Rational thought: "When I look at my life in the big picture, I know I'm worthwhile. One stranger's opinion isn't going to change that."

EXERCISE: IDENTIFY AND COUNTER YOUR ANXIETY-PROVOKING THOUGHTS

Write down three anxiety-provoking thoughts that you might have when meeting a new person. Following each anxious thought, write down a more rational and useful thought that is based on facts.

1. Anxious thought: _____

Rational thought: _____

_____

2. Anxious thought: _____

Rational thought: _____

_____

3. Anxious thought: _____

Rational thought: _____

_____

HOW TO BEGIN A CONVERSATION WITH A STRANGER

Take a tip from Sam. Don't waste time trying to think of the perfect opening line. If you do, the chance for making contact will come and go before you have said a word. Research shows that as long as your opening isn't negative, what you first say to a stranger is relatively unimportant. If the other person wants to talk with you, he or she will respond with something you can use to further the conversation (Garner 1997).

The best way to start a conversation is to say something about the other person or about the situation you both are in. You can show interest in or involve the other person by asking a question. When you ask a question, try to make it open-ended like the ones that Sam asked. Open-ended questions invite others to express themselves at length. This gives you more information, which you can then use to discover mutual interests.

The easiest and least threatening way to start a conversation is to ask a question or make an observation about the situation in which you are both in. Look around and find something that is interesting or puzzling to you, and then come up with a question or a statement of your opinion based on your observations:

- At the grocery store: "I see you are buying those green things that look like grapefruit but aren't. What do they taste like? How do you prepare them?"

- At a party: "What do you think of this music . . . food . . . view . . . house . . . wine . . . ?" Or, "How do you know the host?"

■   To a neighbor: "Your trees are beautiful. How did you get them to grow like that?

■   In class: "What do you think of this class . . . topic . . . teacher so far?"

People are usually pleased to talk about themselves. Take a few minutes to size up the other person. What are they wearing, doing, or saying? What would you like to know more about?

■   "I notice you are reading the new Danielle Steele novel. What's it about?"

■   "Those are really comfortable-looking shoes! Where did you get them?"

■   "I overheard you say that you didn't want the road to the coast widened. Why is that?"

You may want to be more direct in communicating your interest in someone: "You look terrific and I would kick myself if I left here tonight without talking to you." Or, "I've noticed you here before and I thought I would come over and meet you." This direct approach lets the other person know that you are definitely interested and makes a greater impact than more subtle questions or statements.

EXERCISE: CREATING OPENING ONE-LINERS

Think of a recent social situation that you attended. Choose someone you wanted to meet but didn't approach. Make up some opening one-liners that you could have used. Think of three one-liners about the situation and three one-liners about the person you are interested in.

Three one-liners that have to do with the situation:

1. _____

_____

2. _____

_____

3. _____

_____

Three one-liners that have to do with the person:

1. _____

_____

2. _____

_____

3. _____

_____

Practice making up these one-liners in your head when you are in social settings until you are ready to practice them in real life.

HOW TO USE FREE INFORMATION

Free information is what other people tell you that you didn't know before. If you recognize and respond to this free information by making statements or asking questions, you can move the conversation into areas you never dreamed of. Say you are a man wanting to meet a female classmate. You could open a conversation with, "What do you think of this class?" Your classmate responds, "I love it. I'm nuts about European history. I want to go to Europe this summer if I can save up enough money." At this juncture in the conversation, you get to choose which topic you are most interested in learning more about. For example, you could ask your classmate what in particular she likes about European history, how she became so interested in it, where she plans to go in Europe, or how she plans to make enough money to get there. You can either follow up on a piece of free information immediately or come back to it later. While you may want to explore one topic in depth, rarely does a conversation stay on the original topic for long.

Free information includes more than what the other person says. It may be what the other person is wearing, his or her physical features, or behavior, and the context in which you are talking. Free information may also be your general impression of the other person. For instance, you might notice that a person is highly energetic or happy or knowledgeable in some specific area and comment on this.

EXERCISE: USING FREE INFORMATION TO PROMOTE CONVERSATION

In response to each of the following examples of free information, come up with at least two questions and/or statements to further the conversation.

1. "I'm currently unemployed."

_____

_____

_____

2. "I've lived here all my life."

_____

_____

_____

3. "I come out to the beach to surf every chance I get. It beats sitting in front of a display designing circuits all day."

_____

_____

_____

Here are some examples of possible statements and questions:

1. "What did you do when you were working? If you could have any job you wanted what would it be? If you were independently wealthy, what would you do? I've been unemployed before too. I liked the time off. What's it like for you?"

2. "What's it like for you to have grown up and lived in the same place all your life? What do you think the advantages (disadvantages) are to always living in the same place? Where would you live if you could live anywhere?"

3. "I tried surfing once and almost drowned. How did you learn to surf? What do you like best about surfing? What are the circuits that you are designing used for? What's it like being an electrical engineer?"

There are many reasons why people may not respond to your initial efforts to get a conversation going, most of which have more to do with them than with you: they want to be alone, they're shy, or they're waiting for someone else. Remember that it ultimately takes two people to have a successful conversation. Pay attention to the other person's response to you. When people say very little or don't answer your questions at all, when they keep looking away, when they frown, or when they shift their body away from you, it is likely they are not interested. Politely excuse yourself and move on. There are plenty of other people who will be interested in talking with you.

ACTIVE LISTENING

When you actively listen, you listen carefully and you reflect back to the speaker what you think his or her message is, as well as how you think the speaker is feeling. You use active listening when you want to let the speaker know that you are interested enough to listen carefully. You can also use it to confirm or clarify your impression. Refer to chapter 1 if you need help with listening.

GIVING COMPLIMENTS

People want to be appreciated, so it stands to reason that if you want people to like you, you need to let them know what you like about them. Research shows that you are more likely to be perceived by others as understanding, sympathetic, and attractive if you compliment them (Garner 1997). Look for things about people that you honestly like so that you can begin to create an open and supportive atmosphere in which others feel safe expressing not just the facts but also their feelings, opinions, problems, and dreams.

Here are five steps for delivering a successful compliment:

1. **Begin by saying the other person's name.** People like to hear their names spoken.

2. **Be direct.** Praise in a straightforward way what you like about their behavior ("That was a great dinner you cooked") or their possessions ("That's a nice boat you have") or appearance ("You look great in that color!").

3. **Be specific.** You can make your praise more believable by volunteering details about what you admire. Rather than vaguely complimenting the chef, you could say, "Ann, that steak was just the way I like it: pink on the inside and well done on the outside."

4. **Your nonverbal communication should match your words.** For example, give your compliment with a smile and with an upright, open posture, as you say, "Monica, the green of that sweater brings out the green in your eyes. Good choice."

5. **Follow up your compliment with a question if the person doesn't offer free information or dismisses the compliment.** Monica might reply to your compliment to her: "This old thing, I've had it forever. I think it's a hand-me-down from my sister." To help Monica accept your praise, you might add to your compliment, "I always associate people with your coloring with the Irish. What is your ancestry?" When you receive a compliment, be sure to say, "Thank you," and offer some free information related to the compliment.

EXERCISE: PRACTICING GIVING COMPLIMENTS

Think of a person you would like to compliment. Write down three compliments: one about the person's behavior, one about the person's possessions, and one about his or her appearance. Follow the four steps for giving compliments. Imagine the person's response. When you are ready, practice giving compliments in real life.

Compliment the person's behavior: _____

_____

_____

Follow-up question: _____

_____

_____

Compliment the person's possessions: _____

_____

_____

Follow-up question: _____

_____

_____

Compliment the person's appearance: _____

_____

_____

Follow-up question: _____

_____

_____

TALKING ABOUT YOURSELF IN AN INTERESTING WAY

While people like to talk about themselves, they also want to get to know you, so they can decide what kind of relationship they can have with you. What do you believe in? What are your interests and concerns? Where do you live? What kind of work do you do? What do you do for fun? What is your history and what are your dreams? How available are you for future contact? It's not enough to just share facts about yourself. To make facts come alive for your listener, put yourself into the story you are telling by including your opinions and feelings about the facts. For instance, the bare facts are, "I went hiking on Saturday." You might add, "I literally got dizzy sniffing all the different kinds of wild flowers. After being cooped up all winter, I feel like I could fly. I love springtime!" See chapters 2 and 3 for assistance on how to disclose information about yourself as you get to know new people and how to share your opinions, feelings, and wants, as well as the facts.

EXERCISE: PRACTICE TALKING ABOUT YOURSELF

Pick an event from your day or something about yourself and mentally rehearse giving someone an interesting account. Remember to put yourself into your story and share your feelings and opinions as well as the facts. Then actually share your account with someone.

NONVERBAL COMMUNICATION

Nonverbal behavior tells others how you feel about what you are saying or hearing. For instance, the statement "nice hair cut" means different things, depending on your tone of voice (sarcastic versus sincere) and your facial expression (smile versus grimace). Typically, your face tells others what emotion you are expressing, while the rest of your body indicates how strongly you feel your emotions. If you think something is mildly amusing, you smile. If you think it's uproariously funny, you laugh out loud and your whole chest moves.

Crossing your arms or crossing your legs away from the person with whom you are talking indicates that you are tense or uninterested. Tapping or fidgeting can be signs of nervousness or impatience. Uncrossed arms and legs crossed toward the other person or slightly open signals that you are relaxed and interested. Facing the other person and leaning forward shows that you are fully involved in the conversation. Keep in mind that body language can fool you. For instance, the person you are talking to may cross his or her arms because it is cold or may just do it out of habit.

People typically like about three to five feet between them and a stranger, and one and one-half to three feet between them and a friend with whom they are conversing. When you move in closer, you imply that you're interested either in being intimate or are being hostile. When you move farther away, you're implying you're not interested. If you are from different cultures, establishing a mutually comfortable distance between you and a new person can be tricky. For instance, a southern European's personal space is likely to be different from that of a northern European's. A good rule of thumb is to be sensitive to how people respond when you move closer or farther away from them. For instance, if you and another person are standing, move a step closer. If you find the other person backing up, don't automatically move closer to close the gap. The other person may simply be establishing a comfort zone with you, or he or she may not be interested in continuing the conversation. Look to other nonverbal and verbal information to determine which is the case.

Here are some other important nonverbal cues to pay attention to when you are conversing. A warm, firm handshake is the safest way to touch others you are just getting to know. When you are talking, making eye contact for at least one to ten seconds at a time lets other people know that you are interested. You can look at them even longer when you are listening. In Western culture, a single nod indicates that you agree. Repeated smaller and slower nods communicate that you understand and want the other person to go on. Repeated faster nods show that you understand, agree, and want to interrupt. No nods indicate you disagree, are confused, or are uninterested. If you frequently touch yourself, run your fingers through your hair, smile or move about, it's usually a sign that you are interested, nervous, or excited.

EXERCISE: OBSERVING NONVERBAL COMMUNICATION

Go to a party, a restaurant, a school function, or other social gathering and observe people talking with each other. Pay attention to their nonverbal communication. Notice how multiple nonverbal signals go together to convey a message. Write down what you observe:

_____

_____

_____

_____

EXERCISE: OBSERVING NONVERBAL COMBINED WITH VERBAL COMMUNICATION

In a social group setting where you can clearly hear what people are saying, observe how people's nonverbal signals fit or conflict with what they are saying. Write down what you observe:

_____

_____

_____

_____

_____

EXERCISE: PRACTICING NONVERBAL CUES

Choose several nonverbal cues to convey interest and practice them during a conversation with a stranger. Write down what you did and how the other person responded:

_____

_____

_____

_____

_____

HOW TO SUCCESSFULLY EXTEND AN INVITATION

You have decided that you like someone well enough to want to see him or her again. Here are five suggestions you can use to ask someone to get together with you again:

1. Act on mutual interest. Based on your active listening, pick an activity that the other person has expressed an interest in and that you would like to do too. If, for example, the other person likes tennis and so do you, suggest playing a game together.

2. Start small. People are much more likely to agree to do something that doesn't take much effort or time and that sounds safe. For example, they are more likely to meet you at a tennis court that they often use than to drive two hours to another tennis court.

3. Be specific. Suggest an activity, a day, a time, and a place: "Let's get together for a set of tennis this Saturday at the Burgess Park tennis courts in your neighborhood. I could meet you there at ten in the morning."

4. Point out that it's an opportunity for a good time. Based on what you have already learned about the other person, you can suggest how much fun you will have together. For interest, you might say, "From what you have told me about your tennis playing, I think we are pretty evenly matched. I'm sure that it will be really fun to play together."

5. Use nonverbal communication. Look the other person directly in the eyes, smile, and use a tone of voice that conveys excitement and anticipation and reinforces your words.

EXERCISE: PRACTICING EXTENDING AN INVITATION

Think of a person whom you would like to meet again. Using the five guidelines above, write out an invitation you might have made when you met, and then imagine yourself back in that situation, actually inviting them.

_____

_____

_____

_____

If Your Invitation Gets Turned Down

Just because someone says no to your invitation doesn't necessarily mean that they don't like you. They just may not care for your invitation. When this is the case, people usually give an explanation for declining. You can then work out alternative plans. Even if someone doesn't give you an explanation, it is still worthwhile suggesting another activity or time.

When the other person continues to decline without an explanation, you can assume that he or she is not interested. You can graciously end the conversation in a number of ways: "It has been a pleasure talking with you. It's too bad you can't make it." You can also leave the door open to future contact: "Here's my number. Give me a call if you would like to get together some time." You can mention another commitment as your reason for ending the conversation: "I promised the babysitter I would be home by ten. It's been a pleasure. Goodnight."

EXERCISE: PRACTICING GETTING TURNED DOWN

Sousha has invited Diedre over for a study date on Thursday night. Diedre has refused, saying that she has other plans. If you were Sousha, what would you say next?

_____

_____

Carol has invited Patty out for coffee and suggested three different times this week. Patty has graciously declined, but without giving a clear explanation. If you were Carol, what would you say next?

_____

_____

Possible responses:

Sousha: "I could also do it on the weekend. I'm pretty flexible about when we get together. When would be good for you?"

Carol: "Well, I've enjoyed our conversation. I hope we get a chance to talk again sometime. See you later."

This chapter taught you some skills that can help you initiate and carry on conversations with new people. As you practice these skills over time, you will be rewarded with increased ease in meeting new people, enjoyable conversations, and the opportunity to start satisfying relationships.

CHAPTER 12

Discussing Sex: Getting Past Inhibitions and Communicating Your Needs

There are tremendous advantages to being able to talk freely and honestly about sex with your partner:

■ You get your own sexual needs and desires met more often.

■ You know with more certainty that you are satisfying your partner.

■ Your relationship becomes more intimate and enjoyable.

Despite these advantages many couples find it difficult to talk about sex. Some people were shamed at an early age by parents for using sexual language or for asking curious questions about sex. As adults, they still feel an echo of the same shame when they try to discuss sex. Others hold back because they fear rejection. The fear is that if they make their sexual desires known, their partner will turn them down or criticize them. Some people worry that expressing their low opinion of their sex life with their partner will sound like complaining, and they refrain from saying anything to avoid hurting their partner's feelings.

Some people have trouble finding the right words to use to describe sex. Should you be clinical and talk about vaginas and penises? Should you be cute and use the terms common in your childhood? Or should you try the casual, slangy approach and use locker room terminology? At other times, the best words are not enough. So much of sex appeal is non-verbal. It depends greatly on appearance, body language, caresses, scents, grooming, clothes, and so on.

Sometimes sex is difficult to talk about because there is a strong power differential between you and your partner—one of you desperately wants what the other would rather withhold. This makes it very difficult for the person in the one-down position to initiate a conversation about sex.

THE THREE DARK MYTHS OF SEX TALK

The worst impediment to clear sexual communication is believing in one of these three dark myths of sex talk: Perhaps no other area of human relations is so shrouded in myth and mystery as sex. Some of the most limiting sex myths are those surrounding whether, how, when, and to whom you should talk about sex.

Myth 1: Sex is natural and will take care of itself. According to this myth, we are all hard-wired to reproduce as freely and easily as bunnies, and if we just let nature take its course, everything will work out. We shouldn't have to talk about such a natural, simple act.

Myth 2: You shouldn't have to talk at all. According to this myth, you should be sensitive and considerate enough to understand and satisfy each other without having to talk about it. You should just know what your partner wants through a kind of empathic telepathy.

Myth 3: Sexual conflict means the relationship is over, no use talking about it. According to this myth, it doesn't do any good to try to talk through sexual misunderstandings. If you and your sexual partner are in conflict about sex, it automatically means that the relationship is doomed.

The good news is that these *are* myths—they are false ideas that can be dispelled by understanding the corresponding truths about sex.

THE THREE REASSURING TRUTHS ABOUT SEX

It's comforting to know these three facts:

1. Sex is complicated but fixable.

2. You'll never understand and satisfy each other unless you talk about it.

3. Sexual conflict means it's time to talk.

Sex is complicated but fixable. The idea that sex will naturally take care of itself seems plausible only in the early days of a relationship, when you both are eager to please and be pleased. In the honeymoon phase, you both magnify the positive and ignore the negative in a way that often makes sex seem effortless and magical. As time goes on and the rose-colored glasses come off, the little differences and frustrations become more apparent. It's good to know at that point that with communication you can keep your sex life alive and thriving.

For example, Gladys and Roger had great sex for the first three months they were together, then the frequency tapered off a bit. At first, Gladys liked Roger's athletic body and the way he smelled when he'd been working out. Then her innate delicacy reasserted itself. She started pretending to be already asleep when Roger came to bed late smelling of stale sweat from handball on Wednesday and Thursday nights. Roger felt rejected and frustrated, because he was wide awake those nights, pumped up and in the mood for love. It took Gladys several weeks to work up the courage to just ask him to shower before bed on handball nights. He started taking showers, and their sex life got back on track.

You'll never understand and satisfy each other unless you talk about it. Human beings are complex, and human sexuality is much more than just a biological process. Your sexuality is sensitive to many psychological and interpersonal factors, such as beliefs you learned in childhood, your past sexual relationships, and health problems or other possible stressors in your life. It takes two people communicating openly to sort out this kind of complexity. Empathy alone won't do the job.

For example, Bert and Sisily had drifted into a rut. Neither one wanted to initiate sex. Bert felt that he usually initiated sex, and it would be nice for a change if she made the first move. Besides, it had been so long, he didn't want to look desperate. Sisily's Mom and sisters had always told her not to be forward with men, and she would never make the first move. She was worried that Bert didn't find her attractive anymore, and that if she made the first move in bed, he would reject her in revulsion. Their mutual silence and lack of understanding kept them in the rut until one night Bert found Sisily crying and she blurted out, "You never touch me, you think I'm ugly." Once the subject was opened, a few words cleared up the misunderstanding.

Sexual conflict means it's time to talk. When your sex life is on the rocks, it doesn't necessarily mean the relationship is over. It means it's time to talk. This is the most difficult truth to live up to. It's much easier to chicken out and leave or let the relationship drift along. Rather than seeing conflict as the beginning of the end, see it as the beginning of positive change.

For example, Karen liked oral sex, but she knew Paul didn't care for it much. So she never asked for it. She fantasized about breaking up and finding someone who liked oral sex as much as she did, but she never did that either. Paul often felt that he had less sex drive than Karen. He felt pressured to perform sometimes, but didn't want to voice his lack of interest. He thought maybe he would be more interested if Karen wore something sexy once in a while, but he was afraid to ask. They both needed to speak up about their desires, and give the other a chance to please and be pleased. When Karen and Paul finally started talking, they found that the differences between them were much easier to resolve than either had imagined.

FACING GUILT AND FEAR

Guilt is often what robs people of the courage to speak up about their desires. In this case, you feel undeserving of the pleasure your crave, ashamed that you should want to do or experience things that your early training may have told you were sinful or deviant.

Fear of rejection or ridicule is the other common block to asking for what you want sexually. You are afraid that your partner will say no, laugh, think less of you, or comply in a half-hearted, embarrassed attempt to humor you.

EXERCISE: EXAMINING YOUR GUILTS AND FEARS

Write here what you have wanted to do or experience sexually, but have never or seldom asked for because of guilt or fear. Remember that you don't have to show this to anyone. This list is just for yourself, so allow yourself to fantasize freely.

_____

_____

_____

_____

_____

Remind yourself that sex between consenting adults is okay as long as no one gets hurt. That includes all the make-believe, toys, or unusual positions that your imagination can devise.

EXERCISE: EVALUATING LIKES AND DISLIKES

In the following columns, write down the sexual activities you enjoy and don't enjoy and their frequency in your sex life. This will give you a snapshot of how your sex life looks now, compared to how you would like it to look.

Current Sex Life			
Activities You Like	Frequency	Activities You Don't Like	Frequency

Previous Sex Life with Current Partner, If Sex Life was Different			
Activities You Like	Frequency	Activities You Didn't Like	Frequency

Previous Partners			
Activities You Like	Frequency	Activities You Didn't Like	Frequency

Now, write down your fantasies—things you'd like to do or experience, either for the first time or more frequently (surprise, romance, dominance, submission, toys, dress up, new positions, language, role-playing, setting, stripping, oral sex, and so on):

_____

_____

_____

EXERCISE: WHAT'S STOPPING YOU?

In this exercise, identify the impediments you face that keep you from the kind of sex life you desire. The categories below are intended to get you started, but you can use a separate sheet of paper and write about your issues in whatever way seems best.

Your beliefs about sex: _____

_____

_____

Your guilt about sex: _____

_____

_____

Your fears about sex (including fears of partner's reaction): _____

_____

_____

Your stressors (money, health, in-laws, kids, age, non-sex disagreements): _____

_____

_____

What is one thing your partner could do differently that would make a big difference to you?_____

_____

_____

What is one thing you could do that you suspect might make a big difference to your partner?_____

_____

_____

GUIDELINES FOR EFFECTIVE SEXUAL COMMUNICATION

Here are some guidelines for proposing a change in your sexual relationship:

1. Prepare. You have already started by doing the above evaluation exercises.

2. Ask for permission to talk. Don't just spring the subject after years of avoiding it. Tell your partner, "I'd like to talk to you about sex. Is this a good time to talk?"

3. Lead with the positive. Say, "I like it when we do this . . ."

4. Frame your request as an "I message." Say, "I would also like to do this . . ."

5. Avoid using "You messages," such as, "You never touch my penis." This is blaming and will scuttle the conversation right there.

6. Employ active listening when your partner responds. Be prepared for your partner to object or argue. He or she may have several catastrophic "what if" fantasies that need to be clearly defined. For example, "What if I give you oral sex? I'll choke to death" or "What if we agree to see other people? You'll find someone new and dump me" Your partner may reveal hidden resentments or unexpressed wishes, such as, "Why have sex more often, when you just rush through it?" Or "You never just hold me, why should I touch you more?" Respond by paraphrasing and acknowledging your partner's objections until you are sure you understand them and they are out in the open.

7. Stay focused. Don't let the conversation wander into the past or on to other topics such as the kids or finances.

8. Ask for an experiment. This is an important idea that will diminish the threat of a novel request. Ask your partner to try your idea for a night, a week, or a month. By placing a time limit and framing the request as an experiment, you can make the change a collaborative effort that is open to further modification if either of you doesn't take to the new activities.

To make the proposed experiment more enticing, offer a sexual trade or exchange in which you agree to do more of something your partner likes in exchange for agreeing to the experiment.

Deirdre's Story

Deirdre was a morning person. She got too sleepy to make love after ten at night. Her husband Jack loved to stay up late watching talk shows and old movies. By the time he got to bed, Deirdre was fast asleep. When she wanted to make love in the morning, Jack wanted to sleep in. Here is how Deirdre proposed a change in their sexual relationship:

1. Preparation: In her evaluation exercise, Deirdre identified that the one thing her husband could do that would make a big difference would be to come to bed early once in a while. To get him to do this, she was willing to take the initiative in sex, which she found difficult.

2. After dinner, well before bedtime, she said to Jack, "I've been meaning to talk to you about sex. Can we talk now?"

3. She lead with a positive remark: "I always like it when we make love. You still turn me on after all these years, and it makes me feel close to you."

4. She used an "I message" to form her request: "In fact, I would like to make love more often, but I can't stay up as late as you can."

5. She avoided using "You messages," such as, "You never come to bed on time."

6. When Jack protested that he needed to unwind with his late-night shows, Deirdre employed active listening and said, "I realize you need to unwind, and that late at night is the only time you have to be alone."

7. The conversation started to veer off into a discussion of how busy their lives were, with the kids and the business. But Deirdre stayed focused on the sex by saying, "Let's just talk about the time it takes to make love. I only need twenty minutes of your undivided attention, out of three or four hours of television programs."

8. She proposed this experiment: "Not every night, but once in a while, let's try this. I'll come sit next to you on the couch on my way to bed, put my arms around your neck, and say, "I *really want you to* come to bed with me now. That's your signal to turn off the TV and come make love. I don't care if you pop up right after and go back to the TV. That's okay." Jack agreed to try Deirdre's idea, and it worked well. Sometimes he did return to the TV after making love, and other times he dropped off to sleep snuggled in her arms.

EXERCISE: WRITE YOUR PROPOSAL FOR SEXUAL CHANGE

Use this space to write out your own proposal for sexual change.

1. Preparation: What could your partner do for you? _____

_____

What could you do for your partner? _____

_____

2. How will you ask for permission to talk? _____

3. What will be your positive lead in? _____

_____

4. How will you phrase your "I message" request? _____

_____

5. What will be your partner's probable objections? _____

_____

6. How will you acknowledge these objections? _____

_____

7. How will you refocus? _____

_____

8. How will you ask for an experiment? _____

_____

_____

SPECIAL EXERCISES

How is your sexual vocabulary? Some couples have trouble talking about sex because they don't feel comfortable using or hearing certain words for sex acts or parts of the body. For example, Ben hated it when his girlfriend Belinda referred to his penis as "Little Willie," and she cringed every time he used the term "vagina." He thought she was too cutesy, and she thought he was too clinical.

Take the time to agree on a set of terms that you are comfortable with. Every couple should make up their own sexual vocabulary over time, with all the pet names, circumlocutions, or shock value that makes them comfortable and turned on. Discuss these terms together and find out what turns each of you on and off. You may find that you prefer more refined vocabulary some times, and raunchier terminology other times.

EXERCISE: FOCUSING ON SENSATION

If you and your partner learn more about each other's bodies, you will become better lovers. Try this exercise as a simple, nonthreatening way to find out which parts are ticklish, which parts hurt, which parts are neutral, and which parts love to be touched. In a warm, private room, have your partner lie naked on his or her stomach. Agree in advance that you are *not* going to make love. This experience is educational only.

Using just your fingertips, give your partner a very gentle massage all over the body. Don't say anything to each other. Rather, rely on subtle, nonverbal cues such as sighs, deep breathing, tensed or relaxed muscles, movements away or toward your hands, and so on. Let your fingertips explore your partner's body and find out what he or she likes.

At the end of fifteen minutes, discuss the experience. Then trade places and repeat the exercise.

EXERCISE: TAKING LESSONS IN LOVE

In this exercise, you *do* want to talk. Tell your partner exactly what to do to please you. Try this with a massage first, then progress to sexual activities. Give a detailed lesson in loving you, step by step. Be specific: what to do, how long, how hard, how fast, when, and where. If necessary, demonstrate for your partner how you want to be touched or guide your partner's hand. Afterwards, discuss the experience. Be sure to ask if your partner found anything surprising, embarrassing, or distasteful. Trade places and repeat the exercise.

EXERCISE: GIVING AND RECEIVING FEEDBACK

Right after making love, take turns telling each other in detail what you liked about the experience, what left you cold, and what you didn't like. Be sure to begin with the positive information about what you liked, then introduce the negative parts. This is a great exercise because it validates the mutual sexual pleasure you can create for each other, and provides good clues for increasing and deepening that pleasure.

As time goes on, remember to tell your partner when you find something especially pleasurable. As you become more comfortable sharing your feelings, you can begin talking during sex, saying things like, "Hey, slow down," or "I like that, do it harder."

EXERCISE: USING PERSONAL SIGNALS

Some people would rather not talk during sex, preferring to let their body language speak for them. If this is the case for you and your partner, you can still communicate by agreeing on personal signals for crucial information such as "Let's have sex!" or "Let's not!" For example, when Haley had her period, she tended to wear sweatpants to bed, a clear nonverbal message to her husband Bill that she was not interested in sex.

In column two below, put your own nonverbal signals for expressing each message in column one, and in column three, put what you think your partner's signals are for the same messages. Have your partner do this exercise on a separate piece of paper. Then compare lists. You may find that some miscommunication has been going on, and that you need to agree on some clearer signals.

Message	Your Signals	Your Partner's Signals
1. "I like that!"		
2. "I don't like that!"		
3. "I want sex."		
4. "I don't want sex."		
5. "I'm not sure, seduce me."		

This chapter has taught you some ways to communicate better about sex with your partner. The chapter assumes that your relationship is open and nondefensive enough for both of you to be willing to overcome initial embarrassment about talking about sex.

While this approach is sufficient to tune up many couples' sex lives, it may not be sufficient if you and your partner have had sexual difficulties for some time, with many built-up misunderstandings, resentments, and disappointments. In that case, you may require the assistance of a sex or couples therapist.

CHAPTER 13

Talking with Children: Understanding Kids and Making Sure They Understand You

Being a parent can be a daunting responsibility. Most parents are able to provide adequately for their children's physical needs (food, drink, clothing, protection from dangerous situations, and lots of cuddles). Emotional nurturing is more complex. It includes providing positive attention and understanding, accepting and respecting children as individuals, soothing their pain, and fostering their self-esteem. Each of these essential elements is shown in the way you listen, the way you express yourself, and the way you approach problem solving. Everything you say to your child communicates a message about your child and about the relationship between the two of you.

Improving your communication with your children will lead to more cooperation from them, a reduction in conflict, and a better, more intimate relationship with them. Most importantly, good communication can lead to happier, more fulfilled children.

LISTENING COMES FIRST

Paying attention to what your child has to say, with the *desire to understand* his or her thoughts and feelings, likes and dislikes, wants and needs, hopes and dreams, fears and fantasies, communicates that your child is valuable and that what he or she says matters.

EXERCISE: LISTENING TO YOUR CHILD

The next time you spend time with your child, set yourself the task of really listening. When your child has something to say, stop what you're doing, get down to your child's level physically, look your child in the eye, and really pay attention. Acknowledge what your child says. Then answer the following questions:

What was happening? _____

_____

What did your child say? _____

_____

What did you learn about your child's thoughts and feelings? _____

_____

What did you learn about his or her likes and dislikes? _____

_____

What did you learn about your child's wants and needs? _____

_____

What did you learn about your child's hopes and dreams? _____

_____

What did you learn about his or her fears and fantasies? _____

_____

How did you respond (what did you do, what did you say)? _____

_____

How did your child respond? _____

_____

How did your child seem to feel about your response? How could you tell? ___

_____

If you're like most parents, you probably found this last exercise pretty difficult. Most people don't listen to children the way they listen to adults. They listen with certain assumptions that come from being older, more experienced, and having already been children themselves. They know their children so well that they assume they know exactly what they feel and need at any time. It's hard to remember that your children are simply smaller human beings with all the rights to feelings, thoughts, needs, wants, likes, dislikes, hopes, dreams, fears, and fantasies that you have. In fact, children can experience these things far more intensely than you might imagine, and ignoring them doesn't make the feelings, thoughts, needs, and so on go away. Ignored, they usually find their expression in misbehavior.

Sydney's Resistance

Six-year-old Sydney had spent the day at her friend Carrie's house and her dad had just arrived to pick her up. Sydney and Carrie had been jumping on the trampoline and were now sitting on the edge, swinging their legs. Sydney's dad knew that Carrie's family had plans for the evening, so he told Sydney to hurry and find her shoes. "I'm not ready to go," Sydney replied, pouting. "I brought your bike so we could go for a ride in the park before going home," her dad encouraged. "I'm tired," said Sydney. "Well, we don't need to ride," said her dad. "I'm thirsty," stalled Sydney. "I've got water in the car," her dad responded. "But it won't be cold," Sydney complained. "Maybe we could find an ice cube to go in the bottle," suggested Carrie's mom. "It won't fit in the bottle," whined Sydney. After almost fifteen minutes, Sydney—plastic cup with ice water held tightly in her hand—finally got into her dad's car and was driven away.

It probably seemed clear to everyone that Sydney didn't want to leave her friend's house. But no one was acknowledging her feelings or her needs. No one said to her, "I'll bet you're disappointed (frustrated/sad) to have to leave when you've been having such a good time." No one suggested that the girls take ten minutes to make the transition from playing to saying good-bye. No one asked Sydney, "Would you feel better if we promised to set up another playdate soon?" None of these responses would have guaranteed a different outcome. Sydney would still have had her feelings, and might even still have resisted leaving. But chances are that she would have felt heard and understood.

EXERCISE: LISTENING TO YOUR CHILD'S MISBEHAVIOR

Think about the last time your child misbehaved. Ask yourself the following questions:

What was going on? _____

_____

What did your child do? _____

_____

What might your child have been feeling or needing?_____

_____

Did your child try to express these feelings or needs? How? _____

_____

What was your response? _____

_____

How did your child seem to feel about your response? How could you tell? _____

_____

How might you have responded differently? _____

_____

EXPRESSING YOURSELF

People express themselves all the time. On a fundamental level, everything you say, every action you take, is driven by your needs, both physical and emotional. Therefore everything you say and do directly or indirectly expresses something about who you are in terms of your likes, dislikes, thoughts, feelings, wants, and needs. To be the most effective parent, it's essential to be aware of the major rules for expressing yourself.

Andrea hated it when her ten-year-old son, Ryan, left his shoes and jacket lying on the kitchen floor after school. If she put them away for him, she felt resentful. On the other hand, if she left them there, she had to step over them several times in the course of preparing dinner. Although she'd yelled at Ryan countless times to put them away himself, and threatened dire consequences if he didn't, nothing changed.

The best way to engage your child's cooperation in making changes is to express how you feel about the offending behavior and what you want done about it. As a rule, children don't want their parents to be unhappy. They may be unaware of the impact of their behavior on you, or the pursuit of their own needs may simply take precedence over their consideration of your feelings. When you express what you feel and what you want and need, you give your child essential information. With that information, your child can decide whether to keep doing the behavior in question or whether to make other choices.

Three steps are essential in expressing yourself to your child:

- Describe the situation.

- Use an "I statement" to describe your feelings.

- Describe what you want or need in the situation.

Describe the Situation

The first step in expressing yourself is to describe the situation, giving the information necessary to explain why it's a problem for you: "Peter, the dog's dish is empty and he hasn't been fed all day"; "The peanut butter and jelly jars are on the counter, Carol, with the lids off, and the ants are starting to gather"; "Rory, it's almost noon and we're due at rehearsal at twelve-fifteen." Notice that all these descriptions begin with a statement of the situation followed by an explanation of why the situation is a problem.

Sometimes just describing the situation is enough to solve the problem. Peter might decide to feed the dog when he realizes the situation. Carol might put away the peanut butter and jelly—especially if she's going to want an ant-free sandwich tomorrow. Rory might not want to be late to the rehearsal, since he's the soloist.

EXERCISE: DESCRIBING THE SITUATION

How could Andrea have described the situation to Ryan? _____

_____

Possible answer: "There are shoes and a jacket lying on the middle of the kitchen."

Think about some recent incidents with your own child(ren). Use the space provided to write brief statements describing the situation as if you were talking to your child.

Incident 1: _____

_____

Incident 2: _____

_____

Incident 3: _____

_____

Use an "I Statement" to Describe Your Feelings

The second step in expressing yourself to children is to use an "I statement" that owns or takes responsibility for your feelings, such as "I'm really frustrated about something." The alternative is to blame the other person with a "you statement." "You statements" are statements of beliefs, thoughts, or judgments that displace the responsibility for your feelings onto the other person: "You make me so frustrated"; "You're an ungrateful brat"; "You never pay any attention to my needs." Notice how blaming and attacking they sound. Recast as "I statements"—"I'm so frustrated"; "I feel hurt and unappreciated";

"I feel ignored"—they are less offensive and provocative. These are more mature responses, and they are much more likely to be heard.

"You statements" can easily be disguised as "I statements." "I feel that you are behaving like a spoiled brat" is really a "you statement" in disguise. The phrases "I feel like . . ." and "I feel that . . ." are good clues that what follows is likely to be a disguised "you statement." True "I statements" begin with "I feel" and then continue with a word that describes an emotion, such as *happy, sad, depressed,* or *excited.*

EXERCISE: CHANGING *YOU* TO *I*

Recast these "you statements" as "I statements."

1. You really make me angry when you say that.

"I statement": _____

2. You never think before you act.

"I statement": _____

3. You're so thoughtless and unfeeling.

"I statement": _____

Possible answers:

1. "I feel really hurt and offended when you say that."

2. "I get really terrified when you do something that I think is dangerous."

3. "I feel unappreciated and taken for granted."

Describe What You Want or Need in the Situation

The third step in expressing yourself to children is to describe what you want or need in the situation. Sometimes this step is unnecessary. That is, by the time you've described the situation and your feelings about it, the problem is resolved. When that doesn't happen, it's important to be clear about what you want or need in the situation.

EXERCISE: DESCRIBING YOUR WANTS OR NEEDS

Reread the situations above about Peter's dog, Carol's peanut butter and jelly, and Rory's rehearsal, and write brief, clear statements expressing what you as this child's parent might want or need in each situation.

Peter's dog: _____

_____

Carol's peanut butter and jelly: _____

_____

Rory's rehearsal: _____

_____

Possible answers:

Peter's dog: "I would like you to feed the dog when you get home from school."

Carol's peanut butter and jelly: "I want you to put the food away after you use it."

Rory's rehearsal: "I'd like to leave as soon as possible."

In the original story, Andrea had never actually expressed herself to Ryan. She'd threatened and blamed, but Ryan had long since learned to tune that out. So Andrea decided to carefully script what she wanted to say to Ryan and try it out. The following afternoon, she had her opportunity. She described the situations and then expressed her feelings. "Ryan, your jacket and shoes are on the kitchen floor. I feel really frustrated when I'm preparing dinner and I have to step over them every time I want to get something out of the fridge. At the same time, I feel exploited and resentful when I think that you expect me to put them away for you." To Andrea's surprise, Ryan picked up his jacket and shoes with a brief "sorry" and disappeared with them down the hall to his room. Andrea didn't have to explicitly tell Ryan what she wanted. He understood and complied.

EXERCISE: DOS AND DON'TS IN EXPRESSING YOURSELF

There are many common mistakes that parents make in expressing themselves to their children. You can avoid these mistakes and make your task easier by concentrating on certain dos and don'ts.

Dos

Try to achieve the following goals:

Be Clear

It's essential to be clear about your thoughts, feelings, wants, and needs, without leaving anything out or beating around the bush. It's also important to differentiate between your thoughts, feelings, wants, and needs. When a mother says to her son, "I feel like this is a big mistake and you're heading into trouble again," she's confusing her thoughts—"I *think* this is a big mistake"—with her feelings. Her statement might be more clearly and accurately rephrased like this: "I *think* this is a mistake. I *feel* really anxious. I *need* you to explain again why you think it's important that you do this."

Some people are afraid to say what they really mean, and therefore drop hints or talk in vague, abstract terms. "I want you to set the table for dinner and help clear the dishes away afterwards" is much clearer than "I want you to help out more." "I'd like you to bring me a glass of water when you pour one for yourself" is less vague than "I'm so thirsty I could die."

Write an example of something you could say to your child that would be clear:

_____

_____

Be Honest

Being honest means stating your true feelings and needs without fear of upsetting the other person. For example, when you're feeling exhausted and want some time to rest, don't say that you'd really like to help out with your child's homework but you have too much cleaning to do.

Likewise, don't say that helping out at your child's school went "just fine" when actually you felt criticized the whole time. And don't say that you're feeling a little sick and need your daughter to stay home and watch the younger children when actually you're feeling anxious about the party she was going to attend.

Write an example of something you could say to your child that would be honest:

_____

_____

Be Consistent

Especially when talking to children, it's important that what you say and the way you say it don't give two different messages. Your posture, tone of voice, gestures, and so on should match the content of what you're saying. When someone casually asks "How are things?" the typical response is "Fine." Yet many different meanings can be conveyed in that single word with different tones of voice, expressions, and gestures. If things really are fine, your cheerful, positive tone would convey that message. But compare these other messages, conveyed in the same two-word response:

You could say in a martyred tone, "(sigh) I'm fine," implying "actually I'm not well at all, but I'm not worth worrying about."

You could say with frustration, "I'm *fine*," implying "and I'm feeling really annoyed by your constant asking."

Or you could say flippantly, "I'm fine," implying either "don't take me too seriously" or "I don't really want you to know how I am."

Sometimes inconsistencies or incongruities between verbal and nonverbal messages indicate that you don't really know how you feel. Maybe you aren't consciously aware of how frustrated, angry, or resentful you are. If you find yourself giving contradictory messages, you may need to take time out to determine how you actually feel, and then practice conforming your gestures, tone of voice, and posture to fit that feeling before discussing the issue with your child.

Write an example of something you could say to your child that would be consistent:

_____

_____

Be Appropriate

The expression of your feelings needs to match the strength of those feelings. This is similar to the preceding point about consistency. When you're angry, say so. Don't say you're "a little frustrated." When you're feeling deeply hurt and disappointed, don't say that you're "a little upset." On the other hand, you don't want to say that you're "totally devastated" when you're disappointed that your son got a B on his report card. Don't say that you're "enraged" when you're frustrated that your daughter is ten minutes late. Appropriateness refers to nonverbal communication as well: your tone of voice, posture, gestures. Violent behaviors are never appropriate, for example, screaming, hitting, throwing things. The value of finding the appropriate expression of your feelings is that the risk of acting out those feelings is greatly reduced.

Write an example of something you could say to your child that would be appropriate:

_____

_____

Be Immediate

When you have a feeling that needs to be expressed, don't wait until tomorrow or next week. This is especially true with children. Young children have very limited memories and are very present-time oriented. Therefore, they probably won't remember what happened last week, even if it was important to you, unless it was also particularly significant to them. Furthermore, children learn by association. This means that they learn things that are closely associated in time. For example, suppose your four-year-old behaves badly at a social event and you say nothing, waiting until a "more appropriate" time. Then the next day, when she's coloring, you remind her of the event and tell her how upset you were. Because of the delay, your words probably won't have much meaning to your child. In fact, if she feels bad as a result of your words, she's more likely to associate the bad feelings with her coloring than with yesterday's event.

When the behavior is common for your child, you can plan a response and wait for the behavior to occur again. But when it does, you need to say your piece immediately.

Saying right away what you feel in response to misbehavior gives your child the opportunity to immediately adjust his or her behavior. Not expressing your feelings may just cause them to smolder and grow. They may then come out later in an unprovoked explosion or in subtle, passive-aggressive ways. Either way, the relationship will lose.

Write an example of something you could say to your child that would be immediate:

_____

_____

Be Supportive

Remember that your intention in expressing yourself is to be heard and understood, not to get even or prove yourself right. This means trying to express your feelings honestly without being deliberately hurtful. Say your son is almost an hour late from his friend's house, and you've gone from being irritated that he's late again to being terrified that something's happened to him. When he finally turns up, you feel tremendous relief that he's alive and then feel tremendous anger. Being supportive means expressing the relief ("I'm so glad you're okay. I was scared that something awful had happened to you.") as well as the anger ("It's upsetting to me that you didn't call"), rather than just blowing your stack ("You're so thoughtless and irresponsible! I'm not going to let you ride your bike to Jesse's house for a month!"). Setting appropriate consequences is a more effective means of deterring negative behavior than losing your temper.

In simple ways, being supportive means phrasing the things you say in the least hurtful way. "I don't think this is going to work" is more supportive than "That's a stupid plan." "I'd prefer to cook it myself" is more supportive than "Your cooking stinks."

Write an example of something you could say to your child that would be supportive:

_____

_____

Don'ts

The following are things to avoid when talking to your child:

Judging. Judgmental "*you* statements" accuse and attack your child. They contain "you're bad" messages. Furthermore, they interfere with the accurate expression of your own thoughts, feelings, and needs.

Give an example of when you tend to judge and how you could refrain:

_____

_____

Labeling. It's okay not to like your child's behavior. It's okay to think the behavior irresponsible, mean, or selfish. However, a statement such as, "You're stupid and irresponsible," is a condemnation of the child, rather than of the behavior. Global labels, such as "lazy," "stupid," "arrogant," "selfish," "worthless," or "irresponsible," are far more hurtful and damaging than an expression of dislike for a particular behavior.

Give an example of when you tend to label and how you could refrain:

_____

_____

Lecturing and moralizing. No one likes to be told they're wrong. Getting lectured about why you're wrong or why you should be doing things differently just makes it worse. Most children rapidly learn to tune out when they hear a lecture beginning.

Give an example of when you tend to lecture or moralize and how you could refrain:

_____

_____

Commanding. Unless you're in the military, chances are that it doesn't sit well when someone orders you to do something. Commands imply a lack of equality and respect in a relationship, and in many people they trigger an automatic refusal to comply. Children are people, too. They don't like being ordered around any more than anyone else does. If you want to foster a relationship of mutual respect and understanding, it's important to use the courteous gestures and phrases that in our society communicate respect. "Could you please pass the water?" is more respectful than "Get me the water."

Give an example of when you tend to command and how you could refrain:

_____

_____

Threatening. Once again, it's important to keep in mind that your intention in expressing yourself is to increase the level of understanding in your relationship with your child. Threats serve no purpose other than to intimidate your child into behaving the way you want him or her to. The more fear there is in a relationship, the less room there is for respect and caring.

Give an example of when you tend to threaten and how you could refrain:

_____

_____

Making negative comparisons. Negative comparisons not only contain "you're bad" messages, they also make your child feel inferior to others. "Why can't you take care of your possessions like Damon does?" "Sarah is always willing to help her mother do the shopping. Why aren't you?" "Why can't you be more like your brother—he's much more cooperative." These are all examples of negative comparisons. Negative comparisons arouse feelings of defensiveness, rather than a desire to understand your feelings and needs and to improve the relationship.

Give an example of when you tend to make negative comparisons and how you could refrain:

_____

_____

Whatever you say or do, you are expressing yourself. However, it's clear that there are ways of expressing yourself that are more likely both to be heard and to engage the cooperation of your child. When you judge, label, threaten, or lecture your child, you are likely to stir up feelings of defensiveness. But when you describe your feelings about the situation using an "I statement," and when you're clear, honest, and supportive, you contribute to the building of a strong and meaningful relationship.

EXERCISE: PROBLEM SOLVING

Jim had had many discussions with friends and other parents about pets before deciding to buy two goldfish for his six-year-old daughter, Renee. Jim had been reluctant to buy any kind of pet, because he didn't want the responsibility of taking care of it. He was busy enough coping as a single father. But Renee begged and begged for a pet, vowing to do whatever was necessary for its care. She was a pretty responsible kid, so finally Jim relented. Renee was absolutely delighted with her two fish.

Initially, Renee took responsibility of feeding the fish very seriously. She would get up before her father had awakened, and after giving the fish their food, would sit in front of the tank and watch them eat, providing a running commentary—to the fish—on their behavior. Eventually, however, she fell back into her morning routine of turning on the TV until her father got up. The fish went hungry. Jim could see the writing on the wall, and he decided that something had to change. He needed to address the problem with Renee.

Here are six steps to problem solving, (adapted from *When Anger Hurts Your Kids,* (McKay et al. 1996):

1. Talk about your child's feelings and needs

2. Talk about your own feelings and needs

3. Brainstorm all possible solutions without judgment

4. Eliminate those solutions that are not mutually agreeable

5. Pick the best solution or combination of alternatives

6. Develop a plan for implementation and evaluation

Step 1: Talk about Your Child's Feelings and Needs.

Unless you really understand what your child wants and needs, you won't be able to find a solution that takes those needs into account. And unless your child believes that you really are interested in understanding his or her feelings and needs—and knows that you're not just giving lip service to the joint aspect of problem solving—then you'll be wasting your time. Don't assume you know. Ask for clarification. And don't use statements that attribute blame to your child for having needs which differ from yours.

Jim and Renee's problem was that Jim didn't want to have to be responsible for the care of the fish and Renee really wanted the fish but seemed to have trouble remembering to feed them. Step one might have sounded like this:

Jim: Renee, I know you've said you love the fish and want them to get good care, but I've noticed that the fish missed their morning feed four times this week. Do you see this as a problem?

Renee: Yes! I want to remember, but I just forget!

What else might Jim or Renee have said:

_____

_____

Step 2: Talk about Your Own Feelings and Needs

Keep the description of your needs brief. Don't try to convince your child that your feelings and needs are more important than his or hers. Use this opportunity to convey the message that both of you have feelings and needs that are valid. Jim and Renee might have continued this way:

Jim: Renee, I feel really bad for the fish. Often they only get fed because I remind you, and I worry that if I didn't remind you, they might not get fed at all. And the thing is, I don't want to have to remind you. I have enough to remember of my own.

What else might Jim have said?

_____

_____

Step 3: Brainstorm all Possible Solutions without Judgment

Once you've clarified each person's feelings and needs, you can begin brainstorming possible solutions. It helps to write down all the suggestions so that they're not forgotten from one step to the next. If possible, let your child come up with the first couple of suggestions, and remember not to judge or criticize any suggestion, no matter how impractical or impossible you think it is. In fact, a few way-out suggestions may introduce a bit of humor into what may otherwise feel like a very serious process. The more potential solutions you can think of, the better your chances of finding one that at least partially meets both your needs.

Jim and Renee might have continued their problem-solving interaction like this:

Jim: Let's brainstorm some solutions. I'll write them down. Let's not decide if they're any good, just list them. Okay? So, what suggestions do you have?

Renee: Well, you could just feed the fish for me! Or at least keep reminding me to feed them. No, I know you don't want either of those.

Jim: It's okay, I'll write them down. Another suggestion is that we take the fish back to the store until you're older.

Renee: No!

Jim: What if you were to make yourself some kind of reminder to feed them? A sign or a picture or something?

Renee: Yeah, or what if I put a lot of food in the tank every few days and then didn't have to worry about remembering in between?

What are some other alternatives:

_____

_____

Step 4: Eliminate Those Solutions That Are Not Mutually Agreeable

The fourth step in problem solving is to review your list of suggestions and eliminate those that *either* of you finds unacceptable. Since you're looking for compromise, you want to consider only those suggestions that both of you can live with. Read aloud each item on your list. If you think one won't work, say so *without criticism.* "I don't think that would work for me" is better than "that's a stupid suggestion." Remember, if one of you wants to eliminate a suggestion, then it needs to be crossed off the list. Justifications are not necessary.

Take this opportunity to explain why you think something might be a good alternative and worth keeping. Your partner in problem solving might not have considered that. If, despite your persuasiveness, he or she still wants to eliminate that alternative, it gets crossed off.

At the end of this step, you should have at least one possible solution that would work for both of you. If not—if all the alternatives have been eliminated—you have two options. You can brainstorm more alternatives, or you can reconsider some of the solutions you crossed off your list. Jim and Renee might have continued like this:

Jim: Okay, so let me read out the suggestions. The first one is that I feed the fish for you. I'm afraid I'm not willing to do that. *(He crosses it off the list.)* The next suggestion is that I keep reminding you to feed them. I don't want to do that either.

Renee: I knew you wouldn't! You shouldn't have bothered to write that down.

Jim: Well, I think it's important to write down everything we come up with during the brainstorming, even if we kind of know that they're not going to work. Now what's next? You make some kind of a sign or picture to remind yourself to feed them. That's okay with me.

Renee: That's okay with me, too.

Jim: Lastly, you give the fish a lot of food every few days, and then don't have to worry about remembering. I'm not happy with that one. Fish can die from overeating. And besides, how would you like it if I made a big bowl of pasta and left it for you to eat for a few days, so I didn't have to worry about cooking?

Renee: Yuck! Okay, cross that off.

What other potential alternatives are left?

_____

_____

Step 5: Pick the Best Solution or Combination of Alternatives

The fifth step in problem solving is to pick the best solution or combination of solutions from the options remaining on your list. You need to have at least one mutually agreeable solution left on your list before progressing to this step. If a variety of options remain, decide together which one you want to try.

Only one option is left on Jim and Renee's list, so their next step would be easy.

Jim: The only suggestion that we both thought was okay is for you to make some kind of sign or picture to remind yourself to feed the fish. Shall we try that one?

Renee: Okay.

Write any alternative solution you might have come up with: _____

_____

Step 6: Develop a Plan for Implementation and Evaluation

First think through the details of how you will put the new plan to work. Then decide how long you want to try it before evaluating its success. It's useful to develop a fallback plan in case the first solution doesn't work. Sometimes this plan may be another alternative on your list (the second-best choice). At other times, it might involve consequences designed by either you alone or in combination with your child.

Renee: How about I go get my markers and make a sign right now? And I could put it right by my bed, so I see it every morning!

Jim: That's a great idea. When should we decide if it's working or not?

Renee: We'll be able to tell right away. But how about we decide next week?

Jim: Okay. And if it isn't working?

Renee: I guess that would mean you'd want to take them back to the store wouldn't it? I'll just make sure that that doesn't have to happen!

Think of an area of conflict you have with your child that doesn't seem to have been easily resolved. Ask your child to set aside some time for joint problem solving and go through the six steps as outlined above.

PICK YOUR BATTLES

Parenting can seem like an endless series of battles over baths, toothbrushing, bedtime, homework, television, and so on. If you can differentiate between which issues are really yours to address and which really belong to your child, your job as parent will be a lot easier. For example, when your six-year-old wants to wear her pink striped T-shirt with her orange and black polka-dotted skirt, can you let it go? What about when your ten-year-old wants to get his ear pierced and you think piercings are for girls? Can you tolerate your eight-year-old decorating her room with pictures of her idol Madonna? Even though you probably have really strong feelings about these things, they're not really your issues, they're all decisions that your child should be trusted to make.

Reserve your battles for issues that have health and safety implications, or that interfere with your own needs. For example, if your ten-year-old isn't doing her chores around the house, leaving more work for you, that's an issue worth addressing. If your four-year-old constantly interrupts you when you're on the telephone, it's your needs that are being thwarted. If your eleven-year-old keeps climbing on the roof and throwing acorns at passersby, you need to step in.

WHEN YOU HAVE TO SAY NO

Sometimes it's necessary to say no to your child. Instead of saying it directly, you can say it indirectly. There are four ways of setting limits without actually saying no.

Give a Choice

Kids like to feel in control of at least some aspects of their lives. Giving them a choice: "Do you want your bath before or after dinner?" works better than "No, you can't play with the blocks. You have to have your bath."

Substitute "Yes" for "No"

Instead of saying no, qualify the answer with the conditions necessary to get to yes. Say "Yes, you can watch TV, as soon as you finish your homework" rather than "No TV. You haven't done your homework."

Give Explanatory Information

Children are often being told things that make little sense to them ("If you're cranky, you must be tired," or "No, you're not tired, you just woke up"). Giving them information that helps them make sense of a decision will make that decision more palatable. Instead of "No, you can't climb the rope," say, "The top of the rope is all frayed. It could break and you could get really hurt." Say, "I know you wanted to go to Sara's for a sleepover, but it turns out that Grandma Rena is coming to visit and it's been ages since she saw us."

Accept Feelings

We all feel better when our feelings have been acknowledged. Accepting your child's feelings, "I know you really wanted to take your boogie board out again. It's disappointing to have to leave before you feel ready" may take away the sting of the limit.

EXERCISE: SAYING NO

Using the four strategies above to say no indirectly. Write your responses to the following requests.

1. Give a choice in response to "Can we play a game of chess?"

Your response: _____

_____

2. Substitute "yes" for "no" in response to "Can I go to the park?"

Your response: _____

_____

3. Give explanatory information in response to "Can I invite Danny over today?"

Your response: _____

_____

4. Accept feelings in response to "Can I go skiing with Cindy's family?"

Your response: _____

_____

The key to success when you communicate with your children is practice. Children are very forgiving; if they can see that you're trying to improve your skills, they won't condemn you for making mistakes. And if you do make a mistake, don't worry, you'll have plenty of other opportunities to get it right.

CHAPTER 14

Talking with Teens: Bridging the Generation Gap

Talking with teens can be difficult because they are going through a time of life when feelings and opinions run strong. The need for teens to differentiate themselves from their parents can create a generation gap that seems impossible to bridge. To compound the problem, parents who are worried about their teens' safety and future often communicate in prying, manipulative, or blaming ways that they would never employ with other adults. Add the typical family history of past misunderstandings and fights, and it's a wonder that parents and teens ever make contact at all.

The basic communication skills that you learned in the first half of this book apply as much to teens as they do to everybody else. You need to be an active listener. You need to disclose appropriate personal information about yourself. You need to express your thoughts, feelings, and needs effectively. You need to control excessive emotions and be sensitive to the power differential between yourself and teens.

On the other hand, teens can seem like a separate species, requiring a special set of skills. They can be very emotional or very reserved. Teens are very sensitive to hypocrisy or covert agendas. They place a high value on truth and honesty. With teens, certain topics are going to come up over and over— clothes, music, friends, sex, TV, homework, and so on. You need to be able to talk about these things openly, honestly, consistently, and at an appropriate level for the age and personality of your teen.

WHAT ARE THE ADVANTAGES OF TALKING?

It's worth the effort to make contact with the teens in your life. Talking with teens on a regular basis has many advantages:

- You could save a life if the teens in your care hear what you have to say about drinking, drugs, responsible sex, and safe driving.

- Talking will make all the relationships in your family closer and your home life more harmonious.

- Talking now will safeguard your future relationship with your teen, when he or she grows up and you have a more adult-to-adult relationship.

- When you talk with your teen, he or she feels understood, supported, and part of a family and community. Teens who feel this way are happier and do better in school and in life.

EXERCISE: HOW WELL DID YOUR PARENTS COMMUNICATE?

In the list below, rate how well your parents communicated with you on these topics:

Topic	Mother			Father		
	very well	okay	poorly	very well	okay	poorly
their hopes and fears						
their feelings						
their love for you						
their needs						
your clothes						
your homework						
your music						
the movies you liked						
television you watched						
your room decor and cleaning						
money						
your hair						
curfew						
your friends						
tattoos or piercings						
sex						
alcohol						
drugs						
driving						

EXERCISE: HOW WELL DO YOU COMMUNICATE?

In the list below, rate how well you communicate with your teen on these topics. Make a copy of the form for each of your teenage children.

Topic	very well	okay	poorly
your hopes and fears			
your feelings			
your love for them			
your needs			
their clothes			
their homework			
their music			
the movies they like			
television they watch			
room decor and cleaning			
money			
hair			
curfew			
friends			
tattoos or piercings			
sex			
alcohol			
drugs			
driving			

GUIDELINES FOR TALKING TO TEENS

How do your communication skills compare with your parents? In what areas are you improving on the previous generation? Where do you need to do better? Here are some guidelines:

Listen. Most teens clam up around adults. You will have to be a skillful listener to get anything out of your teens. For most adults, the difficult part of listening to teens is listening without judgment. Parents forget their listening skills and jump in with advice, corrections, instructions, and so on.

Ask questions. You have a right to know where your teen is going, who will be there, and what they will be doing. As a parent or guardian you are legally required to know whom your child is with and how to contact your child. Being willing and able to ask good questions will help keep you in touch with your teen and keep your teen safe.

Start slowly. Talk about neutral topics at first, such as movies or music or where to go on vacation. When you have established some rapport and trust, move on to the more contentious topics, such as hair, curfew, sex, and drugs.

Pick your battles. Some issues are not worth going to war over. Depending on your standards and your child's personality, you may have to give in on matters of taste such as hair, clothes, music, TV time, movies, and video games. Harping on these things, after it is clear that your kids aren't going to change, does nothing but create bad feelings and low self-esteem. As your child enters the later teens, you may also find it a waste of breath to preach about staying up late, getting homework done on time, creepy friends, tattoos and piercings, exercise, and good nutrition. Save your waning energy and influence for life-and-death issues such as drunk driving, sex, truly dangerous companions, and drugs.

Walk your talk. Teens have excellent bullshit meters. They can detect hypocrisy a mile away. If you don't walk your talk and practice what you preach, teens will call you on it every time. You can't expect them to behave one way if you behave the other. For example, Grace routinely lied to or withheld information from her kids, doling it out on a "need to know" basis. Then she would get furious when one of them lied to her. If you drink to excess, drive too fast, or sleep around, how can you ask your teen not to do those things?

Be honest. Honest people tell the truth and keep promises. If you can't do that for your teen, you can't really communicate at all. For example, when Bart was teaching his son Randy how to drive, Randy ran over a flowerbed in the parking lot where they were practicing. Bart promised not to tell anyone about it, but he couldn't resist telling his brother Jim. At a family reunion, Uncle Jim brought up the flowerbed episode in front of Randy and Randy's new girlfriend. Randy was so upset that his dad had betrayed his confidence that he wouldn't speak to him for a week.

Do not ridicule or criticize your teen's appearance, behavior, or opinions. For many sensitive teens, there is no such thing as "just kidding" or "constructive criticism."

Say yes as often as possible. Say no carefully, after consideration and discussion, and stick to it. Don't get talked out of a no.

EXERCISE: LISTENING, ASKING QUESTIONS, AND HANGING OUT

For one whole day, stop saying all the automatic things you usually say: the nags, reminders, probing questions, moral exhortations. Just shut up for a while and listen. Listen to your teen, and respond actively with paraphrases, questions, and so on. See chapter 1 for basic instructions on active listening.

Resist the urge to chime in with your own ideas and advice. Draw your teen out at every opportunity. Put all your own agendas and issues on hold for a day. You might enjoy the change in atmosphere so much that you will want to extend the exercise for several days.

If your teen is withdrawn, a day won't do it. You may have to spend a few weeks on this exercise. You may have to create a space for talk: take a trip together, see a play, start a project together, have more sit-down family dinners. If possible, have a weekly time to get together when you can talk away from home. You need to do this more anyway as your teen grows, to counter the natural tendency of teens to disengage.

To get teens talking, avoid what has not worked in the past. For example, don't say, "How was school?" They'll just say "fine." Break the ice with a simple yes/no question: "Is this a better week at school?" Then follow up with "why?" Once you get them going, avoid most simple yes/no questions. Keep asking "why?" and "how come?" You can say, "Tell me more."

If you have tended to be quiet about your own life, it may help to volunteer your own stuff: "When I was in school, I hated gym too." Talk about your own week rather than interrogating your teen about his or hers. On the other hand, if you have overused the phrase "When I was your age," give the memories a rest for a while.

At first, avoid topics that you know might start a fight. Stick to the family pet, favorite foods, movies, or whatever constitutes a neutral topic in your family. Invite objective analysis about a shared experience: "I thought the symbolism in the second *Matrix* movie was heavy-handed" or "What do you like about this song?"

Remember that your goal is to listen, hang out, and just talk. Be very zen about this: Stress the *process* of hanging out and talking, not the *product* of how much information you can extract. Gradually you will find out what your teen thinks and feels about a wider range of topics.

Spend some time listening to yourself as well. While your teen is talking, tune into your own mind. Notice what you want to pounce on and examine. Notice where you want to warn or give advice or make a rule. But resist the urge to steer the conversation around to your own agenda. Remind yourself that you are just hanging out.

EXERCISE: WORKING ON SELF-EXPRESSION WITH TEENS

To establish a baseline for communication, you should pay attention to the kinds of things you habitually say to your teens in your home. For several days, before going to bed, write down what you said to whom during the day:

To this teen	I said

How much of what you say is meant to control your teen's every move? How much is meant to make your life easier or meet your needs? How much is critical, angry, sarcastic, or disrespectful? How much is habitual nagging? How much is clear, uncontaminated communication?

Clear, clean communication is important. You need to put your habitual nagging and covert agendas on hold and practice talking in complete statements that say exactly what you think, feel, and need.

HOW TO TALK IN COMPLETE STATEMENTS

Chapter 3 covered how to compose complete statements, or whole messages. Basically, you need to separate the components of what you want to say to your teen into what you think, what you feel, and what you need. When your statements are clearly divided into opinions, feelings, and needs, you avoid contaminating your messages with the hidden agendas, anger, and blaming that turns teens off.

For example, when Betty wanted to confront Miranda about her curfew, she separated her conflicting thoughts, fears, and desires like this:

Opinion: "I *think* that a fifteen-year-old girl should be home by nine o'clock on school nights and ten-thirty on weekends."

Feeling: "I get *very worried* when it's eleven o'clock and you aren't home yet. I'm afraid you have been hit by a car or something."

Need: "I *want* you home on time. If you're going to be late by even a minute, I want you to call me."

EXERCISE: COMPOSING A COMPLETE STATEMENT

Pick your teen and a topic, and write the complete statement you would like to get across:

What you think: _____

What you feel: _____

What you need: _____

FAMILY MEETINGS

Family meetings are formal encounters with your teen. You can use a family meeting to set limits or devise a more workable living arrangement for your family. The family meeting creates a safe space for communication. Here are the elements:

1. **Make a date to talk.** Don't spring the topic like an ambush. Say "I'd like to sit down and talk with you about your grades. How about after school this afternoon?" You need to make your teen understand that this will be a safe space for him or her to talk. You may have to offer blanket amnesty to get the conversation started: "Whatever is going on at school, whatever is causing the low grades, I promise I won't punish you or get upset. I just want to talk about it calmly and figure out how to solve the report card problem together."

2. **Lead with praise.** Mention something positive that you appreciate about your teen, even if it's no more than "Thank you for agreeing to talk with me. I really appreciate your willingness to talk about this." This is the time to say, "I love you and care for you. I only want the best for you. I respect you as an individual human being, not just as my kid."

3. **Acknowledge past conflicts.** If the topic is loaded with conflict, you may have to apologize for your own past errors in communication: "I know that I've yelled about the Ds and Fs in the past and upset both of us. I want to let all that go, and I promise I'll work with you calmly this time and won't lose my temper. I know this is hard for us to talk about, but I intend to stay calm."

4. **Make a complete statement** that you've composed ahead of time. Say, "I've been wanting to talk to you seriously about . . ." and introduce the topic. Clearly separate your opinions, your feelings, and your needs.

5. **Ask for a response.** Say, "What do you think?" Remember that your teen is probably not as well prepared as you are. Be prepared for strong emotions, refusals, illogical arguments, ultimatums, blaming, and so on.

6. **Listen carefully.** Paraphrase what your teen says to make sure you understand it. Ask "why" questions to get more information.

7. **Encourage discussion and compromise.** Ask your teen, "What would be a fair solution from your point of view?"

8. **Secure an agreement.** Be sure to come to an agreement before you end the meeting. Say, "If I agree to . . . , will you agree to . . .?"

Here is how Howard prepared for his family meeting with his daughter Melanie:

1. **He made a date:** "I'd like to talk to you about your party last weekend. About Cindy and Paul. Is this a good time to talk?"

2. **He led with praise:** "It makes me feel good to see how many kids like you and wanted to come to your party. You're a good friend to them, and I like most of them too."

3. **He acknowledged past conflicts:** "I know I tend to be overprotective, and sometimes I over-react. So I'm being very careful how I put this."

4. **He made a complete statement. He included his opinion, feelings, and needs:** "I don't think kids your age should drink at parties, and I don't think their parties should go on all night. I was upset and worried when I smelled alcohol on Paul's breath the night of the party, and I was pissed off when I found out that he and Cindy had spent the night in the cabana. If you ever want to have a party here again, I need you to make sure that there will be no alcohol and that everyone will go home when it's time."

5. **He then asked for a response:** "Fair enough?"

Melanie explained the extenuating circumstances. She didn't know Paul brought beer or where he and Cindy had gone. At first she asked, "How can I be responsible for what others do?" Then she agreed that she would not invite friends who she suspected would not honor her parents' rules.

EXERCISE: PLANNING A FAMILY MEETING

Pick a topic that you want to settle with your teen. Choose something small that won't spark a major fight. Plan your family meeting here:

Make a date : _____

Lead with praise: _____

_____

_____

Acknowledge past conflicts: _____

_____

_____

Make your complete statement: _____

    Opinion: _____

_____

    Feelings:_____

_____

    Needs: _____

_____

Ask for a response: _____

SPECIAL TECHNIQUES

Teens are a tough audience with whom you sometimes have to talk about embarrassing subjects. Here are some ideas that can make it easier.

Practice in front of a mirror. Rehearse as you would for a speech to a critical audience. Practice speaking up, enunciating, speaking in complete sentences. Maintain eye contact and speak slowly.

Write it down. Write your teen a letter or email. You can carefully craft what you want to say and get it word perfect. Your teen may also find it easier to respond in writing. When the issues are down in black and white, then you can get together and talk about them more easily.

Write a declaration of independence. Some teens yearn for freedom and independence so strongly that it is a constant source of disagreement. If you have such teens, sit down with them and write a "declaration of independence." Spell out what is teen business and what is still your business. Describe the limits within which your teens can live their own life: curfew, where they can go, what they can do, when they can drive, what they can do to their bodies, how they can dress and talk. Specify which new privileges will be granted at each birthday. Arrange new privileges that can be earned by living successfully within the limits. Agree on which privileges will be lost if they go beyond the limits.

Conduct joint problem solving. Rather than calling a formal family meeting where you lay down the law about homework or TV or playing loud music, invite your teen to a joint problem-solving session. In two columns on a piece of paper, lay out the pros and cons of doing homework on time, watching TV all night, or playing loud music. Have your teen tell *you* the likely consequences of him or her continuing to act in the way that's bugging the rest of the family. Brainstorm a list of possible solutions together, then agree on a compromise.

Let grow and let go. Some parents are overfocused on their kids. They want to be a part of every aspect of their child's life. This can be a good thing in the early years when young kids thrive on adult attention. But many teens don't want to be the main focus of your life. Perhaps it's time to turn the spotlight off your teen, take him or her out from under your microscope. Get a life of your own and let your teen have a life too.

Bring in a mediator. A pastor, school counselor, trusted family friend, or a favorite relative can serve as a mediator to help you and your teen discuss difficult issues. When Darby's son Phillip wanted to quit the private academy in which his parents had enrolled him and go to public school, they had loud family fights for three nights running. A meeting over milk and donuts with Aunt Harriet provided a calm setting for them to talk. Darby was finally able to hear Phillip's side—how unhappy he was with the rich smarties, how he'd do better in a larger, more diverse school.

In summary, communicating with your teen on an honest, open level is never easy, but the rewards are great. With better communication, you will enjoy a closer relationship and have more confidence in your teen's ability to deal with the many challenges he or she will face in the future.

CHAPTER 15

Talking with Elders: Maintaining Contact with Aging Family Members

Susan flies back to Ohio twice a year to see her dad, and twice a year she swears "Never again." Her dad, Bradley, is seventy-nine, hard of hearing but unwilling to get a hearing aid. He tells the same stories and asks the same questions over and over. When Susan tries to help him take care of business, asking direct questions about his health and his finances, Brad is evasive. He doesn't want to "bother" his daughter with his problems. Susan feels a desperate urgency to get her dad's affairs settled, sell the old house, arrange for some kind of long-term care, straighten out his bills, and so on. But she feels shut out, unable to make contact and get a straight answer.

Talking to elders often requires some special communication skills because many elders lose some of their ability to communicate effectively. Physical problems such as hearing loss, stroke, or Alzheimer's disease can directly impair communication. The short-term memory loss and chronic pain that often accompany aging can make communication more difficult. Drug side effects can impair concentration in many ways. Depression, the most common emotional problem of elders, makes talking seem not worth the effort.

Some elders have deeply ingrained habits of poor communication that become worse with age. The simple passage of time can put elders out of touch with current events and changing trends. Finally, many elders simply lack the opportunity to communicate because they have lost many of their friends and relatives through death or separation.

It's worthwhile to make a special effort to communicate with the elders in your life. Among the benefits are:

- helping the elders in your family make decisions and solve problems regarding health care and living situations that will improve their quality of life and yours

- reengaging an elder who has become detached from life

- expressing your love, gratitude, and other feelings before it's too late

- making older people feel less alone and alienated

- learning some of the wisdom that a previous generation has to offer

- possibly turning a distant authority figure from your childhood into a close confidant in your adulthood

MAKING CONVERSATION WITH HIGH-FUNCTIONING ELDERS

High-functioning elders are relatively healthy and independent, with most major faculties intact. They may have some hearing loss, joint stiffness, or shortness of breath, but their health is tolerably good. They may forget things and tend to repeat themselves, but they can readily understand the topic at hand and express themselves competently.

Even so, conversation can lag or fail entirely if you don't recognize and compensate for elders' difficulties in comprehension and expression. Susan's big problem with her dad Brad was that she simply talked too fast, pacing back and forth in front of him in a dimly lit room. Brad couldn't hear half of what she said. Embarrassed and annoyed, he found it easier to evade her questions than to understand and answer them.

Speaking to the Hard of Hearing

A little sensitivity and knowledge goes a long way when you are trying to communicate with someone who has suffered significant hearing loss. Here are some tips, adapted from Dreher (2001).

- Speak from a distance of three to six feet.

- Speak into the good ear.

- Turn off the TV or other competing noise.

- Be in the elder's line of sight, with the light on your face.

- Don't obscure your lips with gestures, laughing, eating, chewing gum, or smoking.

- Speak at a natural rate, slowing down only if you see they don't understand. People speak at an average 160 words per minute, but they comprehend words at 500 per minute. This difference is in your favor.

- Speak slightly louder than normal, but don't shout.

- Use short sentences.

- Rephrase misunderstood phrases.

- Let your facial expressions mirror your meaning.

- Start by stating the topic, to give a context.

EXERCISE: PRACTICE BEING LOUD AND CLEAR

The next time you are talking to an elder with hearing loss, see how many of these tips you can remember and put into practice. Remind yourself to notice the distance, lighting, and competing noises in the situation. Be conscious of the volume, speed, and phrasing you are using. Make your short, simple phrases come in loud and clear.

Getting on the Elder Wavelength

Most elders would love to talk to you, if you'd just take the time to listen and remember a few hints that will put you on their wavelength.

For starters, remember that older people have more history than you. Their memories stretch way back to times before you were born. Talking about the distant past is a pleasure for elders for several reasons. It celebrates their history and reminds them of a time when they were young and vital and in charge of the world. Also, long-term memory persists long after short-term memory becomes unreliable. So ask questions about family history and great world events that they have lived through. Aunt Esther may not remember where she put that letter from the insurance company last week, but she can tell you in detail where she used to hide her love letters when she was seventeen.

Elders know how to do things that modern people don't know how to do anymore. Ask "how to" questions that are relevant to their past expertise. An old uncle who can't hold his own with his nephews on the subject of the Internet can discourse for an hour on how to get up steam in a locomotive. Grandma may never be able to reliably respond to her email, but she can tell you all the tricks she used to teach penmanship to second graders in the '40s and '50s. Grandpa may not know or care how your laser pointer works, but he can tell you how to hand cut a dovetail joint on the drawer of a fine cabinet.

Elders may be more tuned into current events than you realize—especially the current events of your family. Tell an elder about some problem that has come up in your life and ask for advice. You may find that the older generation has some shrewd things to say about your current situation. Like anyone, elders love to give advice. Let them give all the advice they want, and remember that you don't have to act on it.

To keep the conversation going and uncover new information, invite comparison and analysis. Ask leading questions, such as

- What was the best job you ever had?

- Who was the smartest . . . meanest . . . handsomest . . . most famous . . . person you ever met?

- What would you do over?

- What would you not do?

- What do you regret not doing?

- What is the funniest family story?

- Who was the black sheep?

- What advice would you pass on to future generations?

You may find yourself so interested that you want to tape-record your elders or take notes for a living history to pass on to future generations. You might encourage an elder to keep a journal as a basis for a living history.

It's important to suspend judgment when listening to your elders' opinions and advice. Remember that elders formed their values and adopted their attitudes a long time ago. What sounds today like a moralizing patriarch talking was once the proper, polite way to express yourself. For example, MaryAnn had a hard time talking to her aunt Mabel about John, MaryAnn's live-in boyfriend. Her aunt had a positively nineteenth century abhorrence of "living in sin," that blinded her to the deep, loving relationship John and MaryAnn enjoyed. MaryAnn learned to ignore the frowns that crossed her aunt's face every time John was mentioned. She realized that she was never going to change her aunt's mind, so she just accepted the dark spots in their otherwise bright conversations.

Likewise, you may find that forgetful elders ask the same question or tell the same stories over and over. Despite appearances, they are not trying to drive you crazy. You need to develop a short, easy answer to the repeated questions, and resist the urge to scream, "For the umpteenth time . . ." Find a simple, neutral response that you can use to head off the same old story: "Yes, I remember that story—it's a good one."

EXERCISE: ASKING QUESTIONS

In the space below, write a list of questions and topics that you can fall back on when you are talking with an elder in your life. Being prepared with conversational ammunition can change a dreaded weekly visit or family reunion from a tongue-tied ordeal into a pleasant exchange of stories and opinions. Take the time now to have real conversations with your elders. Establishing rapport now will help later, when their abilities to communicate decline and they need help making some serious life decisions.

Questions to ask: _____

_____

_____

_____

_____

_____

Topics to bring up: _____

_____

_____

_____

_____

_____

MAKING DECISIONS WITH ELDERS IN TRANSITION

An elder in transition is someone whose declining health or abilities requires him or her to make a major life change, such as moving to a nursing home or ceasing to drive. Elders often need help at these times because they must make major decisions just when their energy, strength, eyesight, hearing, and so on are compromised. Examples of such decisions are

- making a will or trust

- delegating bill-paying or health-care record keeping

- moving into a child's home, assisted living, or a nursing home

- arranging for home health care

- giving up their driver's license

- granting a power of attorney

- making advance directives about end-of-life care

- managing drug prescriptions and compliance

- planning for funeral preferences, burial, or cremation and disposal of ashes

Guidelines for a Decision-Making Meeting

If you need to make a decision with an elder in your life, don't just bring the subject up suddenly or casually. Set a time in advance so that you both have time to prepare. Meet in a quiet, private place that is neat, clean, and comfortable for you both. Have at hand all the information and records that you might need. A box of tissues is a good idea too, in case either of you get emotional. When you meet, be prepared to state your case in a clear and compassionate manner. Here are some guidelines to remember:

- Speak clearly, slowly, and in simple terms.

- State the purpose of the meeting.

- Use the complete message format: I think, I feel, I want.

- Invite your elder to respond.

- Listen without interrupting or arguing.

- Paraphrase or ask questions to make sure you understand.

- Write the pros and cons down in two columns if it will help clarify.

- Summarize and repeat key points.

- End with an action plan if appropriate.

Duncan met with his father at the dining room table in his father's house. He cleared away the breakfast dishes and had the real estate ads handy. Although he had come to visit specifically to convince his dad to sell his house and move into something smaller, he stated the issue carefully and neutrally.

Duncan: Let's sit down together and talk about whether you should move or not.

Dad: Sure, that's a good idea.

Duncan: Let me just explain my thinking, and then tell me your reaction. I think this house is too much for you to take care of anymore. It's too big, too old, and it needs constant maintenance. With all the stairs, I worry about you falling some day. I picture you on the floor alone, with no one to call 911 since mom died.

Dad: I still get around pretty good. I fixed the garbage disposal just last week.

Duncan: I know, but you're not getting any younger. Every year your arthritis is worse. Jeannie and I would feel so much better if you moved now, while you're in good shape, into something closer to us. Something smaller and safer and easier to maintain.

Dad: I appreciate your concern, but I'm really okay here. I've lived in this house for eighteen years, and I've got time still to decide about moving.

Duncan: I agree you're okay right now, today. That's why this is the time to make the decision, when you're feeling good and have all your wits about you. You don't have to move tomorrow, but I think we should have a plan in place, for when we need it.

Dad: I suppose it doesn't hurt to talk about it.

Duncan: Let's just lay it out on paper. If we put the reasons to move in column A and the reasons not to move in column B, how do they stack up?

Duncan and his dad listed the reasons for moving, pro and con. Duncan brought out the want ads, with comparable houses circled, so they could judge how much his dad would get for the old place and how much he could expect to pay for a smaller place near Duncan and Jeannie.

Dad: Okay, you don't have to hit me over the head with it anymore. It's obvious that the only thing keeping me here is inertia. I'm just used to it, and I hate change.

Duncan: So you agree you should move, you just don't want to. At least not now.

Dad: That's right.

Duncan: So can we agree that you are going to move in the future, say the next couple of years?

Dad: Sure, just give me time to get used to it.

Duncan: Agreed.

By exercising patience and respect, Duncan was able to get his dad to agree to a move. The above dialogue was actually the bare bones of a conversation that had more repetitions and digressions. It takes persistence and tact to help elders make important decisions. Notice that Duncan had to divide what he wanted into two separate issues: the decision to move was made; the exact timing of the move will have to be negotiated later.

EXERCISE: DECONTAMINATING MESSAGES

In chapter 3 you learned how to turn contaminated messages into "whole" messages by carefully separating thought, emotion, and desire. Refer back to that chapter if you need to recall the concept of talking in whole messages.

Read the statements below and decontaminate the messages by rewriting them in the whole message format, as "I think, I feel, I want" statements.

1. "Jesus, Mom, you've paid this phone bill twice, but they're about to turn off the electricity and cancel your health insurance. You're stashing mail all over the place like a pack rat. Are you trying to end up sick in the dark? Just leave all the mail for me to go through. Don't screw around with it."

Decontaminate the message:

"I think _____

_____."

"I feel _____

_____."

"I want _____

_____."

Possible answer:

"I think these bills are too complicated for you to deal with these days."

"I feel scared about your power or health coverage being interrupted."

"I want to help. Just leave all the mail on the desk and I'll pay the bills each week."

2. To a ninety-year-old who is almost legally blind: "Dad, Buddy says you nearly hit some guy in the crosswalk. Do you think you should be more careful about your driving? I mean, maybe only go out in the daytime, for short trips? Take the bus more? Or call us for a lift?"
Decontaminate the message:

"I think _____

_____."

"I feel _____

_____."

"I want _____

_____."

Possible answer:

"I think it's time to quit driving. You can't see well enough any more."

"I feel terrified that you're going to kill yourself or somebody else."

"I want you to give me your keys right now."

3. "Mom, this whole situation is nuts. How can you keep taking care of dad when you need a keeper yourself? I don't know why you can't see the handwriting on the wall. It's plain to everyone else that dad should be in a nursing home. How can you do this to us? How can you do this to yourself and dad? It's irresponsible. It's crazy."
Decontaminate the message:

"I think _____

_____."

"I feel _____

_____."

"I want_____

_____."

Possible answer:

"I think dad is too sick for you to take care of him at home anymore."

"I feel sad when I see you so exhausted, and sick yourself."

"I want to help you find a nursing home for dad, so he can get the care he needs, and you can get some rest."

EXERCISE: COMMUNICATING ABOUT DIFFICULT TOPICS

Write a script to communicate with an older person about an important, difficult topic:

Information and resources needed beforehand: _____

_____

_____

Set the time and state the topic: _____

_____

_____

Your thoughts and opinions: "I think_____

_____

_____."

Your emotions: "I feel _____

_____

_____."

Your desires/suggested solution: "I want _____

_____

_____."

MAKING CONTACT WITH ELDERS IN DECLINE

An elder in decline may have had a stroke, a heart attack, or have been diagnosed with Alzheimer's or Parkinson's disease. He or she may be confused, unable to speak clearly or at all, or suffering from adverse side effects of chemotherapy drugs. Memory and attention span may be severely limited. Painkillers such as morphine may sedate an elder most of the time, making contact difficult to establish or maintain. Here are some guidelines for making contact with an elder in these circumstances:

- Touch the person and say his or her name somewhat loudly.

- Make eye contact.

- Smile.

- Speak loudly, but don't shout.

- Speak slowly.

- Use short, simple sentences.

- Ask clear, yes or no questions.

With stroke victims who cannot speak but have comprehension and some movement, try to establish a code for "yes" and "no"—eyelid blinks, hand squeezes. If your elder has had a stroke, is in the early stages of Alzheimer's disease, or is confused for some other reason, don't assume that his or her nonverbal expressions mean the same as they would in a normal person. For example, a stroke patient may nod "yes" and say "no" simultaneously. Tears or laughter and smiles may not mean what you think they do.

Stick to the basics in what you say: "I love you . . . I'm glad to see you . . . You're looking good today . . . Just try to relax . . . You're doing fine . . . We're doing all we can to make you comfortable . . . I hope you get well soon."

If two-way communication is impossible, tell stories from the past. Relive happier times. Tell what others in the family are doing. Read aloud from a favorite book. Hearing is the last sense to go when people are very ill or dying. Even if your elder is in a coma, assume that he or she can still hear and understand you.

For example, when Jeri's dad was in the hospital after his last stroke, she visited him in the morning and at noon, to help with feeding him. She would walk into the room, shake his shoulder, and call his name. When he made eye contact, she'd say, "Hi dad. Here I am again. Time for lunch. Looks like mashed up meat and potatoes and pudding again. I want you to eat up today." While she tried to get him to eat, she kept up a patter of news about her kids' doings in middle school and high school.

Her dad couldn't respond except in an occasional mumbled phrase. Jeri would paraphrase what she thought he said and ask, "Was that it?"

After a bout with pneumonia, he finally couldn't swallow or talk anymore. Jeri and her family decided to put her dad on hospice care, and she said to him, "I'm going to stop forcing you to eat. I know you don't want the food and can't swallow it. It makes me sad, but I'm ready to say good-bye."

Over the last four days of her dad's life, Jeri said good-bye many times. She read aloud from the Bible and from *Travels with Charlie*, her dad's favorite novel. She retold all the family stories and legends. Most important, she got to tell her dad, "I love you. I've always loved you. I will love you forever and ever."

Talking with elders can be frustrating and difficult, but with patience and practice, you can enjoy conversations with high-functioning elders, support them and help make decisions during transitions, and maintain contact when they begin to decline.

CHAPTER 16

Making a Difference: Communicating in Small Groups

A group occurs whenever three or more people gather. When we think of groups, we usually think of formal groups with specific names, such as the United States Supreme Court or the board of directors of a company, in which the members are elected or appointed to fulfill a specific purpose. But many of the groups to which you belong, and which have a significant impact in your life, are informal groups. People choose to band together in informal groups for entertainment, to learn about a common interest, for self-improvement, to worship, to promote causes, and so forth.

In this chapter you will learn to identify a few of the basic characteristics that define the groups to which you belong. The focus of this chapter is on how task-oriented groups work in order to help you

■ communicate appropriately in the four phases of a task-oriented group

■ recognize the roles of group members which can move the group towards its objective as well as roles that can hinder group process

■ become a more effective leader

WHAT CONSTITUTES A GROUP?

Groups run along a continuum from very formal to very informal. All groups serve some purpose, but within formal groups that purpose is clearly defined. Participants are often appointed or elected. The structure of meetings also indicates the level of formality. Formal groups may have a leader who calls meetings together and defines what to do. They also may have a schedule of regular meetings and a secretary or treasurer to keep minutes and records of expenses. Informal groups may meet by chance or only as needed. Membership and attendance are voluntary, and there may be no identifiable leader.

Consider whether a group to which you belong exists primarily for socializing or for completing tasks. In theory, at least, formal groups are for the latter and informal groups are for the former. In reality, most formal groups have an element of socializing mixed in with getting the job done. Most social groups, no matter how informal, have to accomplish some tasks, if only to decide where to have the next party or how to repair the aging sports court.

Think about how many people are in each of your groups and how the group's size impacts the participation of individual members. Typically if there are more than twelve people, it is difficult for more than a handful of group members to participate. In a class of thirty students, usually only four or five do most of the talking. Research shows that in task-oriented groups, such as a committee called together to solve a problem, an ideal number of members is five to seven. This is enough people to provide a rich mix of ideas and skills, and it is few enough people for all to actively participate.

EXERCISE: IDENTIFYING THE GROUPS TO WHICH YOU BELONG

Think of any collection of people you commonly find yourself with. List at least eight of these groups. The group may have a name, or you can describe its purpose or the occasions when it gets together. List the number of members in each group. Rate the level of formality of each group on a 10-point scale from 1 (very informal) to 10 (very formal). Rate the purpose of the group on a 10-point scale from 1 (very socially oriented) to 10 (very task oriented).

Trish made a list of groups to which she belonged.

Description of group	Number of members	Level of formality	Purpose (Social to task oriented)
volley ball group	16	3	2
extended family	25	4	3
weight support group	30	7	5
Pure Play Incorporated	7	8	7
management team	3	10	8
safety committee	10	8	7
lunch bunch	4	1	1
moving committee	6	8	8

Now you try:

Description of group	Number of members	Level of formality	Purpose (Social to task oriented)
1.			
2.			
3.			
4.			
5.			
6.			
7.			
8.			
9.			
10.			

THE NATURAL HISTORY OF A TASK-ORIENTED GROUP

Task-oriented groups usually have four natural phases: the polite phase, the orientation phase, the role division phase, and the constructive phase (Hopper and Whitehead 1979). In each of the first three phases, the roles that members are going to play in the group become increasingly defined in preparation for the final phase. By phase four, members of a productive work group have developed a respectful understanding of one another and are ready to cooperate for the purpose of achieving the group's stated purpose. Rushing or skipping one of the earlier phases may mean that the issues that would normally be dealt with will come up in the last phase and interfere with the completion of the group's stated purpose. It's important to communicate effectively within each phase so that the group successfully moves through all four phases. Don't be impatient to get to phase four.

Polite Phase

During this phase, group members get acquainted and begin to explore what kind of behavior will work well in this group setting. People are on good behavior as members absorb their first impressions of one another. Some tension may develop as group members begin to figure out what roles are most appropriate for them and how to deal with each other as people. You know this phase is completed when several group members stop talking about personal matters and begin to raise questions about the group's goals.

Orientation Phase

In this stage, leaders begin to emerge and alliances are formed. If a leader was not appointed from the start, the group will naturally be looking for one. To whom do other members of the group turn when important questions are asked. Generally, they will turn to someone who has special knowledge about the subject being discussed, someone who is particularly confident, or someone who is an authority figure. Followers will push the leader to take charge by looking at the leader, reinforcing his or her comments, and by accepting the leader's definition of the group's task.

Alliances are formed between members of the group who share similar views on salient issues. They will also tend to agree with each other on other issues. As they support one another, they feel they can exert greater influence over the group than they would as individuals. Alliances only become a problem when members compete with one another at the expense of getting the task completed.

Role Division Phase

In this stage, group members seek out their roles. Potential *task leaders* make their bid for power by offering their definition of the group's purpose or their recommendation of what should be discussed first. Rivals will question their statements. Arguments are not uncommon at this point, as people attempt to establish their roles. Positions within the alliances also appear. Someone usually emerges as a *spokesperson for an alliance*, while other members wait for the spokesperson to speak and then give that person their support.

Other important roles emerge as group discussion continues. The *court jester*, since medieval times, has lightened up the mood of groups with a joke or eased the tension in the room by stating what others are thinking but are hesitant to say in a humorous way. The *outlander* remains detached as he or she listens to the discussion and then poses important questions, points out the weaknesses in the group's positions, and makes innovative suggestions. The *diplomat* clarifies the areas in which people can agree and seeks compromise. The *social facilitator* pays attention to people's feelings and makes people feel good to be members of the group; techniques include smiling, encouraging people to share their ideas, and praising others for their contributions. In a small group, one member may have more than one role. For example, the social facilitator may also be the task leader or the diplomat.

As certain behavior is reinforced again and again, it becomes fixed. If a member is seen as a leader, group members will support his or her leadership attempts. If a member is seen as an outlander, the group will respect his or her questions and ideas and stop to ponder them. Unfortunately, sometimes groups never get beyond this stage, and group members become trapped in their roles for the duration of the group.

Constructive Phase

For the creative juices of a group to really flow in the constructive phase, role flexibility is crucial. While personal roles still exist, anyone can momentarily take on the function of the social facilitator, or task leader, court jester, outlander, or diplomat, in the cooperative spirit of getting the job done. While people will still disagree, there is mutual understanding and respect for different opinions. Anyone can present facts or suggest alternative plans and opinions to help the group arrive at the best solution. In this phase, members will change their minds about an issue as they consider new information. This is unusual in earlier phases. During this time of productive cooperation, members of the group feel very committed to the task. When the group finally arrives at a satisfactory conclusion, the members of the group will be united in defending it to outsiders.

EXERCISE: IDENTIFYING THE FOUR PHASES OF A TASK GROUP

Think about a recent experience you have had participating in a task group. Describe what was discussed that indicated to you which phase you were in.

Trish described the four phases of the moving committee which her boss asked her to lead. The task was to plan the company's move to a new location.

Phase	What was discussed?
Polite	"Small talk about the lunch we were eating, catching up on each other's day."
Orientation	"After lunch, people started asking what we were supposed to do. They looked to me to answer these questions, since the boss had appointed me to chair the meeting. I shared what he had told me."
Role Division	"I suggested we start by brainstorming a list of what needed to be done, agree on it, and then put the tasks in chronological order. Speedball said, 'Too time-consuming. I can make up that list of what we have to do in fifteen minutes and save us a lot of time.' Jeff, his buddy, agreed with him. Connie and Alice agreed with me. Alice quipped, 'They don't call you Speedball for nothing.' Connie thanked him for his input, and suggested that he lead off the brainstorming with his ideas. Jeff asked what the company was going to pay professional movers to do and what our employees were expected to do themselves. I ended the meeting, saying I'd get answers to their questions."
Constructive	"The following day, while people ate their lunch, I shared what our boss had told me. Group members asked me several questions. Then I got out a chart pad and asked for a list of action items that needed to be accomplished for this to be a successful move. Speedball led off and then others added their ideas. After a lively discussion, the group agreed on the list and then put it into chronological order. Jeff suggested labeling who was responsible for each item, E for employee, M for mover, and O for the office manager. There was some friendly debate about whether the employee or office manager was responsible for some items, but these were easily agreed on. Throughout this discussion, people respectfully listened to different opinions, praised creative ideas, and were willing to compromise. The committee agreed on a plan which I presented to our boss."

Now it's your turn:

Phase	What was discussed?
Polite	
Orientation	
Role Division	
Constructive	

EXERCISE: IDENTIFYING ROLES

List the roles that you and others played in the group you described in the last exercise. Give at least one example of what was said or done that indicated to you that a member had taken on a particular role. Note, a member may have more than one role, especially in the constructive phase. Make up the name of a role to cover the behavior you observed if it hasn't been mentioned in this chapter.

Trish's example:

Role Division	Person	What did they say or do?
Task leader	Trish	Defined the problem and goal and part of the means to attaining it, called and ended the meeting, reported the group's conclusions. Led discussion in the constructive phase. Reported the conclusions.
Alliance spokesperson	Speedball	Dismissed leader's plan. Pushed own agenda.
Alliance supporter	Jeff	Agreed with the alliance spokesperson.
Court jester	Alice	Diffused the tension with humor.
Diplomat	Connie	Acknowledged Speedball's input and suggested a compromise.
Outlander	Jeff	Raising an important question.
Constructive Phase		
Task leaders	everyone	Contributed and evaluated ideas.
Social facilitators	everyone	Acknowledged and praised ideas.
Outlanders	everyone	Raised questions; pointed out weaknesses.
Diplomats	everyone	Looked for compromise.

Now it's your turn:

Role Division	Person	What did they say or do?

Identifying and Dealing with Derailing Tactics

In the last exercise you described the various roles that group members assumed to enable the group to accomplish its goal. You probably noticed behavior on the part of some group members that interfered with the group process. Here are seven actions that members of a group may take that can get in the way of the group accomplishing its task:

1. The *class clown* uses humor to get attention rather than to lift the group out of tense moments.

2. The *traditionalist*, content with the status quo, resists all new ideas.

3. The *victim* complains about how unfair things are.

4. The *cynic* points out how nothing the group is considering will work or make a difference.

5. The *fanatic* holds onto his or her position at all costs.

6. The *perfectionist* gets bogged down in the details, loses sight of the big picture, and is reluctant to reach a conclusion that is less than perfect.

7. *Fence-sitters* hold up the group because they can't decide between equally good alternatives.

EXERCISE: IDENTIFYING ROLES THAT INTERFERE WITH PROGRESS

Draw a line from the role to the example of what someone in that role might say.

Role	What someone in that role might say
1. fence-sitter	A. "I think we need to really research this before we make a decision as to whether to use salmon-colored or apricot-colored paper. Colors really affect people's mood, and there are the issues of cost and availability of the paper."
2. class clown	B. "Why can't we just do it the way we want. Management never lets us be really creative. It's just not fair."
3. fanatic	C. "These forms have done their job for ten years. Haven't you ever heard the saying, 'If it ain't broke, don't fix it?'"
4. perfectionist	D. "I can't believe you're thinking of doing it that way. It's too complicated. Our customers will never figure it out."
5. victim	E. "Salmon is a pretty color, but apricot is so much warmer. While Salmon is cheaper, apricot may be more appealing to our customer, but I'm not sure."
6. cynic	F. "I think it should be plain orange, and that's that."

7. traditionalist   G. "Knock, Knock. Who's there? Orange. Orange who? Orange you going to let me in? Did I ever tell you about the time I drank two quarts of orange juice just before I went sky diving?"

Answers: 1—E; 2—G; 3—F; 4—A; 5—B; 6—D; 7—C

HOW TO STAY ON TRACK

It is challenging for the leader and frustrating to other group members when a group member's behavior interferes with the group completing its task. The best way for leaders to keep the group on track is to be prepared. Here are ten suggestions that you can use as a leader to respond to group members who derail a group. Each suggestion will be followed with an example of how it might be used to respond to one of the statements in the last exercise.

1. Start out by clearly defining the group's task, and periodically restate it. In response to a class clown, you might say, "I need to remind the group that our purpose here today is to decide how to display information about our services to our customers in the lobby."

2. Prepare an agenda and set appropriate limits regarding how much time will be spent discussing an issue. In response to a fence-sitter and perfectionist, you might say, "We have four topics to cover in one hour today, so we can spend fifteen minutes on the color of the paper."

3. Be prepared with information or have access to resources to answer questions likely to come up in the group discussion. In response to a perfectionist and a fence-sitter, you might say, "I borrowed the secretary's office supply catalogue to see what colors of paper are available and how much they will cost. I also brought an old college text that happens to have a chapter on how color affects mood. To save time, here's a quick summary of this material. I'll pass around the resources if anyone is interested."

4. Use reflective listening to acknowledge and clarify what a group member has said. In response to a fence-sitter, you might say, "So you're saying you like both of these colors, but can't make up your mind because you don't know how the customer will like it, right?"

5. Reframe what a group member has said in a positive, accurate, realistic, and balanced way. In response to a victim, you might say, "Management is actually asking us to be creative and come up with a proposal. I know you would like to do something really nice, and it seems unfair that management is limiting how much we can spend. But that's part of how this company makes money to pay our salaries."

6. Acknowledge and explore criticism. In response to a cynic, you might ask, "What is it about the system that we are discussing that would be too complicated for our customers?"

7. Devise a way to test assertions. In response to a cynic, you might say, "That's a good point. Let's be sure to evaluate our new system after the first week it goes into effect to be sure that customers understand it."

8. Explore the basis for a group member's point of view. In response to a fanatic, you might ask, "Why plain orange?"

9. Acknowledge and respect differences of opinion before asking for compromise in the interest of accomplishing the group's task. In response to a traditionalist or a fanatic, you might say, "I admire a person who knows what he wants; but in the interests of getting the job done, can you accept majority rule on this item so we can move on?"

10. Give people enough time to discuss and reflect about the issues and the facts. You may want to circulate an agenda for the meeting to all group members before the meeting so they can do their own research and reflect on the topics before they arrive. You may want to postpone making a decision until after a break or the until the next meeting, so that people have time to think. In response to a perfectionist, fanatic, and fence-sitter, you might say, "Let's take a short break while you look at the catalogues and the chapter on color and think about what you think is best. Then let's come back and make a decision."

EXERCISE: BE PREPARED AS A LEADER

Think of a group in which you will be the leader. List five things you can do to prepare for it.

1. _____

2. _____

3. _____

4. _____

5. _____

EXERCISE: STAYING ON TRACK

Think of a group in which you have been a leader. In the first column, imagine five statements from group members that might derail the group from accomplishing its goal. In the second column, respond to each of these statements in a way that will move the group forward toward its goal.

Derailing statements: **Your response:**

1. _____   _____

   _____   _____

   _____   _____

2. _____   _____

_____   _____

_____   _____

3. _____   _____

_____   _____

_____   _____

4. _____   _____

_____   _____

_____   _____

5. _____   _____

_____   _____

_____   _____

   The next time you participate in a task-oriented group, try to determine which phase the group is in. Notice what roles are being played by which group members. Try to communicate in such a way that you help the group successfully move through its four phases and achieve its objective.

CHAPTER 17

Overcoming Stage Fright: Speaking Effectively in Public

Lindsay had been asked by her research professor to speak at the upcoming annual conference on the research she and her professor had been conducting together. Lindsay was both flattered and terrified. She'd never spoken in front of a group, much less a large group of professionals. She didn't know the first thing about public speaking, and the idea made her quake in her shoes.

Public speaking is different from other kinds of communication and there are many benefits to learning how to present yourself well in the public forum. Knowing the key elements to a successful public presentation can lead to increased confidence when you have to speak. It can also increase your respect in the eyes of your colleagues as well as afford promotion opportunities. Finally, presenting yourself well improves your chances of making an effective speech.

This chapter should be particularly helpful if you are planning to deliver a speech in the near future. It will also be helpful if you have decided against public speaking in the past and you want to get over your stage fright.

HOW PUBLIC SPEAKING IS DIFFERENT

Public speaking is unlike any other kind of speaking. It is usually more formal, requires planning and organization, and generally has a specific purpose. Some speeches are strictly informational. Some speeches are attempts to persuade the audience to think, feel, or do something, such as vote for a particular person, or give money to a specific cause. The purpose of some speeches is to arouse sentiment or passion; the purpose of others is the opposite: to calm or reassure the audience.

It's essential to determine the purpose of your speech before you begin to write. It's also important to decide what kind of presentation you're going to give, based on your knowledge of the material and your understanding of the audience you're going to be addressing.

What Is the Purpose of Your Speech?

Determining the purpose of your speech is of primary importance. Most speeches have as their goal either to inform or to persuade.

EXERCISE: WRITE A CLEAR STATEMENT OF PURPOSE

Imagine a speech that you want to make. In the space provided, write a statement that describes what you want to accomplish in your speech. Do you want to inform the audience with your speech? Do you want to persuade the audience to do, think, or feel something? Try to make your statement of purpose succinct yet comprehensive. Use the space to hone your statement until you're completely satisfied.

Lindsay wrote her first statement as follows: I want to effectively describe the impact of different hormones on tumor growth in mouse ovaries that we've been researching and the new process of measurement we've developed.

Her final statement was: My speech will describe the impact of hormones on mouse tumor development and new methods of measuring tumor growth.

Write your initial statement of purpose:_____

_____

_____

_____

Now write your final statement of purpose: _____

_____

_____

_____

Your Style of Presentation

Unless you know your subject really well and can think on your feet, an *impromptu* speech is not for you. *Extemporaneous* speaking involves adequate preparation without actually memorizing the speech so that you can be organized yet demonstrate spontaneity in how you express yourself. This might include making notes on index cards. Memorizing your speech is likely to produce a mechanical-sounding presentation, and you should probably avoid it. However, for professional talks such as Lindsay's conference presentation (or a political announcement, for example), a *manuscript* speech, prepared and read word-for-word would be appropriate. Lindsay decided to write a manuscript speech, but her eventual goal was to practice it enough that she could eventually speak extemporaneously from an outline.

EXERCISE: DECIDE ON YOUR PRESENTATION

Think about what style of presentation would be most appropriate for your speech.

Write the style of presentation your speech will have: _____

_____

Determine Your Audience

The better you tailor your speech to your audience and their circumstances, the better your speech will be received. Jokes, comments, language, examples, and speech length are all things that you can tailor to the population you're addressing. Are you talking to men or women? Are you talking to teens? Is it going to be warm in the room? Will the audience have just eaten? Or will everyone be hungry? Are people likely to be angry? What are their political affiliations? There are many factors that could influence the impact of your speech and that you should take into account in preparing your presentation. The following is a list of potentially important factors:

- **Gender.** If you're wanting to persuade your audience, knowing that you'll be speaking to all women or all men might influence the kind of language or jokes you use to gain their trust and confidence. Sympathies of men and women are stirred differently as well, so examples used to illustrate your points might be influenced by the gender of your audience.

- **Age.** Older people have different concerns from younger people raising families, whose concerns are different again from single adults with no dependents or from teens facing the challenges of adulthood. You should take these factors into account if your audience is of a particular age.

- **Ethnicity.** Knowing the ethnicity of your audience can help you tailor your speech to gain the group's sympathy and support. How you talk about illegal immigrants, for example, might differ depending upon whether you're speaking to Chinese businessmen or Hispanic farmworkers.

- **Economic status.** People in the upper-income brackets have different concerns from those at the bottom of the economic ladder. Persuasive material needs to take these differences into account.

- **Educational level.** Language that is appropriate for a highly educated group might feel patronizing or too high flown for ordinary people.

- **Occupation.** You can take audience occupation into account as you prepare your speech. For example, eliciting support from employees of a manufacturing plant for a particular political candidate will be easier if you can show that the candidate has supported workers' rights.

- **Liberal or conservative.** General attitude, be it liberal or conservative, can influence how an audience responds to your presentation. A speech on abortion rights for women, for example, would be tailored one way if you are speaking to a liberal group and another way if you are speaking to a conservative group.

- **Attitudes.** Knowing your audience's specific attitudes towards your particular topic can help you approach the presentation differently.

- **Interests.** If you know your audience's interests, you can tailor your examples, jokes, and personal revelations to fit those interests, gaining your audience's confidence that you are like them and therefore worth listening to.

- **Time of day.** If your presentation is first thing in the morning, your audience is likely to be more alert and attentive than right after lunch or at the end of a long day. If your audience is tired, you might try more humor and less heavy detail.

- **Audience seating.** If your audience isn't comfortable, its ability to focus may be reduced. On the other hand, physical discomfort in your audience might facilitate your ability to stir anger or passion—emotional discomfort.

- **Hunger level.** If your presentation is right before a lunch break, you make it brief, focusing only on the essential points.

- **Mood leftover from previous speaker.** If your presentation is scheduled directly after someone who has left the audience angry or hostile, you need to know. That way you can tailor your introduction to acknowledge the situation and provide a necessary transition to your topic.

EXERCISE: ANALYZING YOUR AUDIENCE

Look over the categories below and fill in the characteristics that most accurately describe your audience and their circumstances (to the best of your knowledge).

Gender: _____

Age: _____

Ethnicity: _____

Economic status: _____

Educational level: _____

Occupation: _____

Liberal or conservative: _____

Attitudes: _____

Interests: _____

Time of day: _____

Comfort level of audience seating: _____

Hunger level: _____

Mood from previous speaker: _____

Lindsay filled in the categories to the best of her ability. Since she had no information about when or where in the conference center her speech was going to be presented, she could only fill in about half of the list:

Gender: *Mixed, probably more men than women*

Age: *Adults of all ages*

Ethnicity: *No idea, probably mixed*

Educational level: *Highly educated*

Occupation: *Mostly researchers in the medical field*

Liberal or conservative: *No idea*

Attitudes: *Hopefully positive rather than antagonistic*

Interests: *No idea*

Time of day: *No idea*

Comfort level of audience seating: *No idea*

Hunger level: *No idea*

Mood from previous speaker: *Hopefully interested in what's coming next*

THE OUTLINE

Creating an outline for your speech makes filling in the rest of the material significantly easier. Keep two major requirements in mind when organizing your material: all good presentations have an introduction, middle, and a conclusion; and essential information must be repeated at least three times to be remembered. "Tell them what you're going to tell them, tell them, and then tell them what you've told them" is the common rule of thumb.

EXERCISE: OUTLINING YOUR MATERIAL

1. Take three separate pieces of paper, and write "Introduction" at the top of the first page, "Body" at the top of the second, and "Conclusion" at the top of the third. Write down all the points you want to cover in each section. Remember the importance of repetition, and plan on having your introduction and conclusion sections briefly summarize the main points that you're presenting in the meaty middle (body) section of your talk. You might find it easier to write body first and then complete the introduction and conclusion sections.

2. Once you've finished making notes, you must organize them into a more cohesive structure. There are many models for presenting information depending on the kind of information. Sometimes a sequential or chronological approach works best; sometimes it helps to list different problems and their solutions or causes and their effects. Some information can be best presented as several unrelated topics, or as issues related spatially rather than developmentally. Rewrite your outline using the organizational model you've chosen.

3. Now think about the supporting materials you want to use: jokes, statistics, quotes, illustrations, examples, audiovisual aids, and so on. Make notes on your outline at the points where you want to use some supporting material.

Lindsay's completed outline looked like this:

Title: Impact of Hormones on Mouse Tumor Development

Purpose: To describe the impact of hormones on mouse tumor development
and new methods of measuring tumor growth.

I. Introduction

   A. Systemic exposure to Hormone X reduced mouse tumor size by 50 percent after one week.

   B. Tumor was further reduced 39 percent by addition of Hormone Y.

   C. No effect of Hormone Z, applied alone or in combination with X and Y.

   D. Measurement of tumor size was facilitated by using laser technology.

   E. Implications for the future.

II. Body

    A. Hypotheses

    B. Methodology

        i. Strain and number of mice used

        ii. Method of tumor stimulation

        iii. Selection and production of hormones used

        iv. Method and timing of application of hormones

        v. Control groups

        vi. Attrition of subjects

        vii. Development of laser measurement technique

    C. Results

        i. Tumor reduction for each single hormone research and control group over one-month period. Show graph.

        ii. Tumor reduction in hormone combination groups. Show graph.

        iii. Side effects observed in groups. Show chart.

    D. Discussion

        i. Hypotheses

        ii. Possible explanations of different groups' results

        iii. Implications for future research and development

        iv. Study limitations

        v. Impact of laser measurement technique on current and future research

III. Conclusion

    A. Reduction in mouse tumor size of 50 percent by Hormone X

    B. Further reduction of 39 percent by combination exposures of Hormones X and Y.

    C. Role of laser measuring technique

    D. Implications for future

DELIVERY TIPS

The success of your speech depends on much more than just the content of your presentation. If your voice is monotonous or too soft to hear without straining, you'll lose your audience's attention. If you rush through your presentation or use words or expressions that are too intellectual for people, they'll have to struggle to maintain focus. Finally, if you seem uninterested in your audience, or your presentation seems wooden, the audience's attention will wander. Your voice is key to your delivery. Be sure to

- Present your speech to the people in the back row (or even further back!) of the audience to ensure enough volume.

- Talk more slowly than you think is appropriate. Your audience has to follow and absorb what you're saying and that takes more concentration than simply participating in a conversation.

- Speak clearly, in short sentences, and use terms that are simple yet appropriate to your audience.

- Let your tone vary with what you're presenting; don't talk in a monotone.

- Make eye contact with your audience members.

- Use the personal pronouns "I" or "we" to personalize your presentation and engage your audience.

- Pay attention to your nonverbal signals. Let your facial expressions, body posture, and movements of your arms and hands, support what you're saying. Consider walking around while you talk if it will give your speech vibrancy.

EXERCISE: PRACTICING IN REAL TIME

Using a tape recorder, give your speech as you plan to deliver it to an audience. Listen to the speech and, using the delivery tips listed above, notice where you need to make changes to improve your presentation. Repeat the process, this time watching yourself in a full-length mirror while you record yourself. (A video recorder would work as well). Notice your nonverbal signals and make a note of what you want to change. An alternative option is to practice giving the presentation to a friend and having your friend give you feedback on the areas that need more attention. In the space provided below, outline the areas that you need to focus on:

_____

_____

_____

OVERCOMING STAGE FRIGHT

There are several strategies to reduce stage fright. Progressive relaxation, practiced ahead of time, can be tremendously useful. Visualizing a successful presentation is an important tool. And one of the best antidotes is to do some real-time practicing of your presentation, as described previously.

EXERCISE: PROGRESSIVE RELAXATION

Sit in a quiet place and close your eyes. Focus for a few moments on breathing slowly and deeply. Then go through the following steps, tightening each muscle group for seven to ten seconds and then releasing the tension and relaxing the muscle group for thirty seconds while you breathe slowly and deeply. Focus on the feelings of tension and relaxation.

Muscle groups:

- Wrinkle your face and forehead like a walnut.

- Hunch your shoulders and tighten your neck muscles.

- Take a deep breath and hold it to tighten your chest muscles.

- Clench your buttock and stomach muscles.

- Clench your fists and tighten your forearms and biceps.

- Pull your toes and feet towards your face and tighten your shins and thighs.

- Curl your toes and feet away from your face tightening your shins and thighs.

The more frequently you practice progressive relaxation in the weeks preceding your presentation, the more easily your body will relax at that moment before starting your speech when you take a deep breath and tell yourself to relax.

EXERCISE: VISUALIZATION

Sit in a quiet place and close your eyes. Imagine yourself walking onto the stage to give your presentation. See yourself smile at the audience and take a deep breath. Begin your speech and notice how you're feeling. If there's some anxiety, notice how it soon passes and is replaced by calm, focused feelings. Make eye contact with members of your audience and notice how interested they seem. Continue your presentation and visualize finishing to loud audience applause and signs of approval.

Take a few moments to practice the relaxation described in the previous exercise, then repeat the visualization. Do this until you can go through the entire visualization without anxiety.

Remember to practice your speech, using either a tape recorder, a video recorder, or delivering it to a friend.

Lindsay practiced all three of the exercises to overcome her stage fright. She noticed that eventually she could become fairly relaxed just by focusing on breathing slowly and deeply. Her visualizations felt relaxed and she was optimistic. However, when she started the real-time practice, she was astonished to discover that she spoke much too fast, and that some of what she said sounded garbled on the tape recording. There was also very little variation in her tone. She repeated the exercise and focused on speaking much more slowly and more expressively. The full-length mirror showed even more surprises. Although she felt relaxed, she noticed that, rather than move naturally, she held her body very still as she spoke and that she appeared almost wooden. With additional practice, Lindsay made the necessary alterations and felt confident that she would make her presentation with success.

Regardless of who your audience is or what you're presenting, you can improve your presentation by practicing the tools offered in this chapter.

References

Antony, Martin M., and Richard P. Swinson. 2000. *The Shyness and Social Anxiety Workbook: Proven Techniques for Overcoming Your Fears*. Oakland, Calif.: New Harbinger Publications.

Bach, George. R., and Peter Wyden. 1983. *The Intimate Enemy: How to Fight Fair in Love and Marriage*. New York: Avon.

Black, Jan, and Greg Enns. 1997. *Better Boundaries: Owning and Treasuring Your Life*. Oakland, Calif.: New Harbinger Publications.

Davis, Martha, Elisabeth R. Eshelman, and Matthew McKay. 2000. *The Relaxation and Stress Reduction Workbook*. Oakland, Calif.: New Harbinger Publications.

Dreher, Barbara B. 2001. *Communication Skills for Working with Elders*. 2nd ed. New York: Springer Publishing Company.

Garner, Alan. 1997. *Conversationally Speaking: Tested New Ways to Increase Your Personal and Social Effectiveness*. Los Angeles: Lowell House.

Gray, John. 1992. *Men Are from Mars, Women Are from Venus: A Practical Guide for Improving Communication and Getting What You Want in Your Relationships*. New York: HarperCollins.

Hopper, Robert, and Jack L. Whitehead, Jr. 1979. *Communication Concepts and Skills*. New York: Harper and Row.

Katherine, Anne. 2000. *Boundaries: Where You End and I Begin*. New York: Fireside.

Linehan, Marsha. 1993. *Skills Training Manual for Treating Borderline Personality Disorder*. New York: Guilford.

McKay, Matthew, Martha Davis, and Patrick Fanning. 1995. *Messages: The Communication Skills Book.* 2nd ed. Oakland, Calif.: New Harbinger Publications.

McKay, Matthew, Patrick Fanning, Kim Paleg, and Dana Landis. 1996. *When Anger Hurts Your Kids: A Parent's Guide.* Oakland, Calif.: New Harbinger Publications.

McKay, Matthew, Peter Rogers, and Judith McKay. 1989. *When Anger Hurts: Quieting the Storm Within.* Oakland, Calif.: New Harbinger Publications.

Tannen, Deborah. 1990. *You Just Don't Understand: Women and Men in Conversation.* New York: Quill.

Some Other
New Harbinger Titles

Helping A Child with Nonverbal Learning Disorder, 2nd edition, Item 5266 $15.95

The Introvert & Extrovert in Love, Item 4863 $14.95

Helping Your Socially Vulnerable Child, Item 4580 $15.95

Life Planning for Adults with Developmental Disabilities, Item 4511 $19.95

But I Didn't Mean That! Item 4887 $14.95

The Family Intervention Guide to Mental Illness, Item 5068 $17.95

It's So Hard to Love You, Item 4962 $14.95

The Turbulent Twenties, Item 4216 $14.95

The Balanced Mom, Item 4534 $14.95

Helping Your Child Overcome Separation Anxiety & School Refusal, Item 4313 $14.95

When Your Child Is Cutting, Item 4375 $15.95

Helping Your Child with Selective Mutism, Item 416X $14.95

Sun Protection for Life, Item 4194 $11.95

Helping Your Child with Autism Spectrum Disorder, Item 3848 $17.95

Teach Me to Say It Right, Item 4038 $13.95

Grieving Mindfully, Item 4011 $14.95

The Courage to Trust, Item 3805 $14.95

The Gift of ADHD, Item 3899 $14.95

The Power of Two Workbook, Item 3341 $19.95

Adult Children of Divorce, Item 3368 $14.95

Fifty Great Tips, Tricks, and Techniques to Connect with Your Teen, Item 3597 $10.95

Helping Your Child with OCD, Item 3325 $19.95

Helping Your Depressed Child, Item 3228 $14.95

The Couples's Guide to Love and Money, Item 3112 $18.95

50 Wonderful Ways to be a Single-Parent Family, Item 3082 $12.95

Caring for Your Grieving Child, Item 3066 $14.95

Helping Your Child Overcome an Eating Disorder, Item 3104 $16.95

Helping Your Angry Child, Item 3120 $19.95

The Stepparent's Survival Guide, Item 3058 $17.95

Drugs and Your Kid, Item 3015 $15.95

The Daughter-In-Law's Survival Guide, Item 2817 $12.95

Whose Life Is It Anyway?, Item 2892 $14.95

Call **toll free, 1-800-748-6273,** or log on to our online bookstore at **www.newharbinger.com** to order. Have your Visa or Mastercard number ready. Or send a check for the titles you want to New Harbinger Publications, Inc., 5674 Shattuck Ave., Oakland, CA 94609. Include $4.50 for the first book and 75¢ for each additional book, to cover shipping and handling. (California residents please include appropriate sales tax.) Allow two to five weeks for delivery.

Prices subject to change without notice.